Who Won the Battle of
the Atlantic?

Who Won the Battle of the Atlantic?

Martin T Gilbert

ATHENA PRESS
LONDON

ISBN 10-digit: 1 84748 089 6
ISBN 13-digit: 978 1 84748 089 7

First Published 2007 by
ATHENA PRESS
Queen's House, 2 Holly Road
Twickenham TW1 4EG
United Kingdom

Printed for Athena Press

*This book is dedicated to the men who were boys when
I myself was a boy in wartime Wearside.*

Cover Photograph

This book is about shipbuilding on the River Wear during the Second World War and the very large contribution which the many small yards there made to the war effort. Throughout those difficult years, more ships and greater tonnage sailed from the Wear than from any other river in the UK.

This photograph shows one of the smaller yards which will be familiar to those who lived in Sunderland through the war, as it is clearly visible from Monkwearmouth Bridge in the centre of the town. This view shows Messrs Austins Brothers yard with its pontoon dock in the foreground, the fitting-out quay in the middle and the building ways visible just round the bend at the rear of the photograph and to the right. Because the river is narrow, the launching ways were sited on a bend so that ships could be launched up the river, giving much more space to slow the hull down by the drag chains than would be available directly across the river.

The ship on the pontoon dock is a standard cargo ship of about 4000 tonnes. Across the river, the fitting-out quay of Thompsons yard can be seen; here they built the larger Liberty ships which formed the backbone of the transatlantic shipping replacing the grievous losses of merchant ships on that route.

I acknowledge with thanks the help given by Susan at the *Sunderland Echo* who found this print in their archives. It is post-war because the ships are not all painted grey. I accept with gratitude the permission of the editor to publish it.

Acknowledgements

I would like to thank Amanda Ball of Sunderland University for putting me in touch with the *Sunderland Echo* who kindly provided the cover picture of Austin's shipyard; David Page who allowed me to select warship photos from his site at www.navyphotos.co.uk; and Peter Swarbrick who allowed me to download the enhanced images of those.

The details of ships both in the text and in the image captions were provided by *Jane's Fighting Ships* 1944/45 issue, for which Jane's Information Group kindly gave permission. I also thank Mike Mills of Exeter Reference Library for allowing me the repeated use of that volume and for providing other valued support.

My use of information and opinions derived from the various sources are my responsibility alone.

Contents

Introduction

As in the First World War, the movement of food and weapons from the USA and much of the rest of the world to Europe was of crucial importance from the beginning of the Second World War in 1939. At a later stage the shipping of men and weapons became the essential start of the winning offensives on mainland Europe – it was necessary in 1918 to get American troops on the ground in France. In 1943 and 1944 it was fundamental to the strategy of defeating Nazism that major invasions of North Africa and the mainland of Europe should be possible by sea.

In both conflicts the German Navy used the submarine as its principle weapon in disrupting the seaborne trade, but only after the use of major warships, operating remote from home, had failed to stop the flows from around the world in the face of superior surface forces mustered against them. The struggle to maintain the vital seaborne trade from the USA became known as the Battle of the Atlantic.

It is customary to accept that winning the Battle of the Atlantic was the key to the survival of the United Kingdom as an effective opponent of Nazism, the only one for many years, and many factors contributed to this eventual, hard-won victory. Among these were the dogged determination of the men of the Merchant Navy in the face of appalling losses; the immediate institution in 1939 of protected convoys; and the development of strategies and tactics to oppose the very effective submarine fleet which had, by 1941, brought shipping losses to frightening levels.

Later on came the intervention of air power by the use of Woolworth Carriers to escort specially important convoys and the operations of Coastal Command of the RAF to sink submarines while they were on passage on the surface. All of these activities were made more powerful by the development of new sensors and weapons about which not a great deal was known to the public at the time for obvious reasons. What is strange is the extent to which this lack of knowledge persists today.

What did Sunderland have to do with it?

This book is an attempt to honour the many men and women whose everyday efforts, over many hard years, brought these essential items to bear on the conflict at a critical point in our history, by building and fitting out the many types of merchant ships and warships built on the river Wear. None of them wore uniform; many of them suffered from bombing and displacement; all of them endured rationing, lack of winter fuel, queuing for essentials and family disruption. Furthermore, most of them worked in poor conditions and endured hardships associated with manual labour and the constant blackout.

Their contribution should be recognised whilst some are still with us, as many have already been taken with the passage of time; their successors may need their example in the hard times now threatening from global warming and the widespread conflict of ideas. I hope that this book can help us to understand how things appeared to them when they were making that contribution – without which none of us would be where we are today.

Martin Gilbert
October 2006

Technological Developments

The New Sensors

In examining these, the emphasis will necessarily be upon the seaborne aspects of the battle because, although the airborne war against the U-boat was continuous, its area of effectiveness was very small until late in the conflict. There was a gap of hundreds of miles in the mid-Atlantic until the introduction of the various methods of getting attack aircraft to accompany the convoys began in late 1942 and even then in only a very small way for the most important convoys. For most convoys throughout the war, the defence was carried out by the surface ships of the Royal Navy (RN) and the Royal Canadian Navy (RCN) who detected and then attacked the threatening submarines. After 1942 the US Navy began to exert some influence in the western Atlantic and by 1944 were matching the efforts of the UK and Canadian naval forces combined.

To begin with, the available ships for convoy protection were known as destroyers, a name with historical roots but which bore little relation to the vessels available in 1939. At that time there were many different classes of destroyer from small ones such as the S Class at 900 tonnes, the F Class at 1400 tonnes to the very large Tribal Class at 1900 tonnes, but they all had one thing in common; they were all-purpose ships. They had guns of between 4 in. and 4.7 in. bore, and these were hand-worked in three or four gun mountings with an armoured shield, but open to the elements and frequently washed down by breaking seas. The guns were directed by mechanical computers well below decks and visual sights and rangefinders mounted high in the ships, and most of them would not elevate above thirty degrees.

Many classes, such as the V and Ws, had been built in the 1920s and until quite late in 1940 few of them had specialised anti-aircraft weapons larger than machine guns, although these were sometimes in multiple mountings – a lack which cost them dear against dive-bombers. None of this affected their ability to combat submerged submarines, however. The guns could, and frequently did, sink a surfaced submarine but first the submarine had to be found and damaged badly enough to force it to the surface. Most of these ships could approach 30 kt at full speed – some could reach 36 kt – and mostly they had good seakeeping ability, able to work effectively in good weather and bad.

A strategic decision was made at the end of the First World War in 1918 to augment the destroyer fleet by converting several classes such as the later Vs and Ws to escort ships and to enhance their anti-submarine weapons by adding Depth Charge Throwers.

In 1935 several coastal escorts were ordered such as the Kingfisher and Guillemot classes. These had limited range and a top speed of 20 kt. The Smiths Dock Company developed a design in the late 1930s, based upon one of their whaling ship hulls, for what eventually became the Flower Class corvettes, but no orders were placed by the RN. The RCN, on the other hand, ordered several to be built in Canada in 1939 and the RN also bought some from Canada in 1941, before they were being built in the UK.

The first response by the British Admiralty in 1939 was the panic ordering of fifty corvettes and the immediate purchase of fifty outdated US Navy boats (the Four Stackers as they were known) which, served by valiant crews conscripted in the UK, were a significant help to the hard-pressed, pre-war destroyers. To these were added the corvettes as they were commissioned. They were a smaller, specialised ship of 900 tonnes with a top speed of 17 kt, aimed at long-range convoy protection and which took to sea the latest sensor equipment and some new weapons. These smaller hulls were relatively quick and cheap to build and could be constructed by shipbuilders hitherto unused to Admiralty work and in yards where larger ships could not be launched for lack of water. Their numbers grew to over one hundred as the years passed and in 1944 they were the major convoy protection vessels, and although other ships such as the River Class and the Bird Class sloops were also used as convoy escorts, they were not specialised for anti-submarine work.

Detection of the Target

In destroyers, the method of detection was then known as ASDIC, a device based upon a high frequency sound source which directed a beam into the sea and which recorded any echoes both in the earphones of the operators and upon a paper chart which unwound slowly as the equipment was operated. This was not a new concept, having been developed in 1917 by civilian scientists and engineers at the Admiralty Underwater Weapons Establishment (AUWE) at Portland in Dorset as a successor to the passive listening equipment then used. It was a very potent source of data once it locked onto a submarine target.

In 1939, the standard ASDIC set fitted in destroyers was the 144 which had a rotating head driven by remote hand control by the operator. It would routinely search ahead of the ship, over an arc prescribed by the captain, but it could rotate through the whole circle once without damaging the connecting cables and then reverse and unwind itself and so cover the whole area around the ship.

Was it Effective?

It had several major deficiencies: it had a narrow conical beam, perhaps 50 ft across at a 100 yd range; it had very limited range which depended upon both sea conditions and the operator's ability to detect; and it had a fixed angle relative to the surface of the sea, pointing downwards due to reflections from the sea's surface. Its ability to find a submarine could be likened to the process of trying to find a man in a haystack by poking a thin rod into it and hoping to hit him.

When an echo was received, one of the essential skills of an ASDIC operator was to answer the captain's question, 'Sub or non-sub?' The echo could be from a shoal of fish or from some floating debris, either on the surface or under water. The ASDIC beam could be directed by the operator to examine the target in width but not in height by scanning across it. An experienced operator would know both by the extent of the target at the appropriate range and by the quality of the echo whether or not it was a probable submarine. After that he would try to define its course and speed, from which the team in the operations room of the ship could then deduce a future position for an attack to be directed. If the captain decided to attack, which could depend upon permission from a higher authority who was directing the convoy defence, the ship would then become both the detector and the attacker and would be dependent upon the ability of the operator to hold the target which could, by then, be trying to escape by dodging or going deep to get below the beam. A submarine captain can hear the 'ping' and knows how to escape.

A fast attack, with a good operator working well with a good ship handler is an exciting chase and, with luck, could lead to the cry from the operator of 'instant echoes'. This call meant that the ship was above the submarine and could launch its weapons.

Enhancing the Usefulness of ASDIC

The effectiveness of this rather feeble device could be increased by having several ships on a defensive screen around the convoy, each with an allotted arc of search. Ships had a choice of operating frequencies for their ASDIC transmitters so that neighbouring ships did not interfere with each others' ASDIC, and these frequencies would be laid down by the escort commander at the start of the voyage. The lack of deep water cover could be slightly alleviated, given enough ships, by deploying one well ahead or well astern whose ASDIC beam could cover the area below the convoy from some distance. In good conditions an echo could be expected from a 2- to 3-mile slant range which could be sufficiently deep to cover the area below the convoy but only in good conditions.

One of the major problems for all acoustic systems operating in water is that there are likely to be layers of water at different temperatures below 100 ft; if a sufficiently large difference exists then this layer can reflect the sound beam at the interface so that nothing below the layer will give an echo. Submarine captains can detect this phenomenon and use it as a reliable defence.

There were other limitations in the use of ASDIC. The transmitting and receiving unit was a magnetostriction oscillator, a composite device made up of many quartz-metal discs about

18 in. in diameter. The whole transducer was 6 in. thick and was mounted at the end of a vertical shaft which carried its weight and enabled it to be rotated to different bearings relative to the ship's hull, but it obviously needed to stick out of the bottom of the ship to do that. At a ship's speed of 5 or 6 kt, the pressure on such a disc would snap it off unless the stalk was extremely thick. Supposing that such a strong stalk was practical, then the noise created by the rush of water past such an obstruction would totally overwhelm any possible echo. It was therefore essential for this transducer to be housed in a streamlined casing known as the ASDIC dome, a thin casing which could be lowered below the hull. It was originally named thus because of its shape but now they are almost always of a streamlined shape to minimise the noise of the water being parted by the leading edge and passing along the sides, while creating the minimum wake astern of itself.

The design of a suitable shape is always developing but in 1939 there was a standard shape and size which was fitted to all ships; it was about 6 ft long and 2 ft wide and hung 4 ft below the keel of the ship in its centre line and usually well forward in the hull. However, it could not be too far forward or it would break the surface when the ship climbed over a wave and in practice it was usually mounted 50 ft to 80 ft aft of the stem. Another reason for this position was to further minimise, by distance, the noise of breaking water where the stem of the ship was cutting through the sea – a compromise which could seldom be avoided.

Problems with Acoustic Transparency

There was a further problem: the dome needed to be invisible to the beam of sound so that the maximum power entered the sea and the largest possible echo power was received at the transducer face. In practice this was impossible but the skin was made sufficiently thin and was roughly circular in plan section at its front end with the ASDIC transducer mounted at the physical centre of that circle, so that any attenuation was the same on most bearings. Astern, because of the need to streamline the shape of the dome, the plan shape was attenuated to a point and echoes from astern had errors in bearing because of that. Then again, because the metal of the dome was thin and could not be interrupted by strengthening ribs, it was not very strong and at a ships speed above 10 or 12 kt the dome would collapse. Consequently the dome needed to be raised within the hull for speeds above about 12 kt and this precluded any use of the ASDIC above that speed. When retracted, the bottom of the dome faired into the keel and was strong enough to withstand any manoeuvre apart from grounding. The dome was raised inside the hull into a separate watertight compartment which also housed the transmitter and receiver for the ASDIC. The operator's console was remote from these in a small space just below the front of the bridge so that the officer directing the ship could speak directly to the operator. He could then ask for the echoes to be put onto a loudspeaker on the bridge so that he too could hear it; a skilled ship handler could know almost as much as the operator from practice listening to the echoes.

A well worked-up team could be certain of closing on a submarine once it was detected providing that the submarine did not go too deep or get below a thermal layer in the sea. The skill of the hunter against that of the quarry then determined who would survive the encounter and it is a tribute to the many ships' teams that so many submarines were sunk using this primitive device.

What was Done About It?

All the deficiencies mentioned were well known to the civilian scientists at AUWE and they had designed units to counter many of the known problems even though, until 1938, no money was available for the manufacture of enough kits for improvements to existing ships to take place. Trials of locally manufactured prototypes in Portland had demonstrated the feasibility of these new devices; the first was the Q transmitter which was a small wedge-shaped unit to be mounted below the main round transducer. This gave a secondary beam, narrow in width but with large vertical coverage making it fan-shaped and which therefore could give more precise bearing information about a submarine than the normal search beam, so that the main beam could be brought to bear more accurately on the target.

They had also developed further equipment known as ASDIC type 147, which included a separate special transducer in its own thin casing which projected below the hull and was movable in both training and elevation This also had a fan-shaped beam although this one gave wide horizontal coverage but was narrow in height; this beam could be automatically trained round to the same bearing as the main ASDIC and then traversed in elevation so that a depth could be deduced for the target. Knowledge of both the range and the depth of the target aided the ultimate destruction or damage of the submarine by allowing a more precise depth setting for the weapons and a more accurate heading for the ship at the time of the attack.

After 1938, the fitting of these improved devices was expedited whenever ships came in hand for docking, and by the end of 1940 most escorts were equipped with them. After that the improvements to the ASDIC installations for nearly twenty years were mainly in reliability, better amplification, clarity and display of echo signals, ease of maintenance and a repair by replacement policy for all new production. Because of developments elsewhere it was felt that the ASDIC part of the attack system was doing all that it could do using the available technology and in the face of the inevitable limitations imposed by the nature of the seawater. There was the added limitation of having few knowledgeable people to carry out the research.

What Improvement Did Take Place?

The biggest single improvement in the ability of escorts to detect submarines came not from below the surface but from above it – by radio detection. This was not radar, although in time that had its place; the device involved utilised the ability of the surface ship to hear and to home in on the submarine transmissions. The frequency band in which submarines received their orders from U-boat headquarters in Germany was a very low frequency worldwide transmission which submarines could receive below the surface, not when they were deep, but far enough down to be invisible to surface ships.

What changed was the development by the U-boat command of a wolf pack system of attack upon defended convoys, which was intended to overwhelm the escorts by simultaneous assaults from several directions. It was extremely successful and destroyed many convoys almost totally until a defence was available – the ability to detect the submarines 'chatting' to each other and reporting convoys to their headquarters. To transmit on this band of frequencies the submarines needed to surface and to transmit on high frequency, that is above 3 MHz. The transmissions were coded and were automatically sent at very high speed – a burst of transmission lasting perhaps three or four seconds. The equipment which the civilian scientists and engineers at the Admiralty Signal and Radar Establishment (ASRE) in Portsmouth developed was a high frequency direction-finding set known as HF/DF ('huff duff' to the sailors) and which was designed to be fitted to escort ships. It had a very sensitive, fixed directional aerial looking like a birdcage and which was mounted high on the mast, well above all surrounding metalwork. This aerial had two pairs of very low-impedance cables which led down the mast to a receiver with two channels. The first stage of each channel was a tuned radio frequency amplifier and it was followed by five further stages of intermediate frequency amplification before being used by the operator. Besides his headphones, there was a visual display on a cathode ray tube; if the two-channel amplifier was properly set up and the input stages were tuned to the precise frequency involved, this display would show the transmission from a submarine as a line of light. This light would lead from the centre of the display to a point on the circumference where a graduated ring showed the bearing of the transmitting ship relative to the receiving ship. An operator could therefore detect and note the bearing of these very short transmissions with a fair degree of accuracy. The FH4, as the set was known, was fitted progressively in newly built corvettes from the end of 1941, and by 1944 it was at sea in many other classes of ship as well.

How was the New Ability Used?

The new capabilities enabled individual ships to detect a transmission and to establish the bearing from which it came. A single ship could be ordered by the escort commander to steam down the bearing and sometimes to find the submarine. No range was given by the FH4 equipment but the detection limit was the radio horizon, say 30 to 35 miles at the most, and after unsuccessfully following the initial line for an hour, a single ship would be ordered to rejoin the convoy. If two ships got the same transmission they could fix the submarine within a square mile at a 30-mile range; if three ships got it, the fix would be even closer. The escort commander could then plan his countermeasures instead of having to wait for the first exploding torpedo in the middle of the convoy.

Because of the highly secret decoding operations by the civilian specialists at Bletchley Park, the Admiralty could brief the escort commanders on what frequencies the U-boats were likely to use and arrange for each escort to cover one of them; as soon as any escort got a fix the others could be told of the frequency and so listen out for more transmissions. As previously mentioned, all the U-boats involved would be using the same frequency for a given wolf pack operation, and in this way it became possible to hear the packs assembling and know where they were heading by the changes in the bearings of their transmissions and thus make the necessary moves. These might include rerouting the convoy to avoid the pack or concentrating an escort attack upon the assembling individual submarines before they formed the pack.

On some occasions the intercepted transmission could be decoded by the experts in Bletchley Park and the exact positions passed to the escort commanders. By the beginning of 1942, most escort groups had some ships fitted with the HF/DF and by the end of 1943 all had them as standard. The tables then began to turn and more submarines were being sunk than could be built to replace them. U-boat losses rose from 60 in 1942 to 148 in 1943 and to 158 in 1944.

What is odd is that the German Navy never deduced that this was the method of detection; they believed that a form of radar was involved and used radar-defeating coverings for submarines as a defence. But it was not the sensors alone which brought such successes; the weapons too had evolved and now ensured that more of the U-boats initially detected, whether by radio or by ASDIC, were subsequently sunk.

The New Weapons

Anti-submarine Weapons

From the outset of anti-submarine warfare, the object has always been to cause damage to the submarine hull and equipment to such an extent that it must either surface to survive or is so damaged that it sinks below its crushing depth and becomes a total loss. A submarine sunk in shallow water, less than 100 ft, will be able to save those of its crew who are fit enough to swim up, either with or without breathing apparatus, but it will also be vulnerable to renewed attack from the surface. The standard weapon has always been an explosive charge, sometimes with a fixed time-delay fuse and sometimes with a depth-sensitive fuse, preset to explode at the desired depth.

In destroyers in the First World War a weapon known as the depth charge could contain between 100 and 200 lb of high explosive of various kinds and usually had a depth-set fuse which needed to be turned by hand using a key shortly before release. The charge was contained in a cylindrical steel shell about 18 in. across and 2 ft long; there were smaller ones but that was the standard unit. It was not intended to fracture, so as to produce shards of metal to penetrate the submarine hull, but to produce a pressure wave in the water close to the submarine and so to rupture the hull or to break the feet off equipment so that the submarine installations became unusable. It was especially likely to fracture the many glass cells of the vast batteries on which all submarines depended for their underwater propulsion.

Nevertheless, many submarines survived such attacks unless the depth charge exploded within about 30 ft of the hull or further away if two straddling charges exploded simultaneously. Even a surviving submarine might well be in darkness after an attack and could have multiple minor leaks and extensive machinery damage. The use of more than one depth charge in each attack was usual and there were several different ways of achieving that. The easiest method was to roll the charge out of a railed track on the stern of the ship. In a destroyer with a beam of 14 ft that would mean two charges 14 ft apart which, given the relative inaccuracy of the tracking device, (the ASDIC), was rather like shooting at a sparrow in flight with a small bore rifle with no proper sights.

By 1918, the standard 'depth charge pattern' had been developed which was a ten-charge or eight-charge pattern, and this was achieved by using two types of discharging method. On each side of the deck aft were two mortars, each able to project a depth charge of about 40 ft away from the ship, after which it would sink in the usual way. If, at the moment of attack, with the ship steaming ahead over the top of the target, two charges were rolled off the rails, two thrown from each side and another two rolled off the stern, it was possible to produce a rectangular pattern about 100 ft across. These charges could also be staggered in the depth at which they would explode to give a better spread, but opinions differed about the effectiveness of that and the decision lay with the officer directing the attack. All of the actions, both rolling out and projecting sideways by mortar, were carried out by a timing mechanism whose settings were arranged to suit different ship speeds through the water. The initiating signal to start the pattern could come either from the captain on the bridge, from the torpedo gunner on the quarterdeck or from the ASDIC operator. Different ships developed their own procedures.

At the beginning of the Second World War all destroyers had such depth charge equipment and the differences between various classes of destroyer were mainly in the number of charges which could be carried on board in the magazine. As well as the magazine below decks there were 'ready-use stowages' on deck so that all the rails and the mortars could be reloaded following an attack. However, because of the weight of the charges and the number involved, the time taken to reload in the very confined spaces on the destroyer deck could be twenty minutes or well over that in bad weather. As a result, once one attack had been carried out, the next one could not be carried out until reloading was finished and that could easily allow a submarine to escape a single-ship attack, unless the first pattern had disabled it. The odds against such success were very high, but a two-ship or three-ship attack could make a kill much more likely. There were seldom enough destroyers in any convoy escort for that tactic to be used in every attack, however.

When the Flower Class corvettes were designed they had smaller hulls and could not, therefore, carry as many depth charges, which were heavy and bulky and demanded many cubic feet of space both below decks and on the small quarterdecks. They nevertheless had a small outfit of charges in the rails and mortars and one ready-use reload pattern on deck. The depth charge was a potent weapon against a stopped submarine where an attack at leisure might be possible, but the Flower Class also had a new device. It had many advantages over the depth charge but its main advantage was that it did not require the ship to pass over the submarine before releasing its charges – this one could throw its charges ahead of the ship.

The submarine captains who could not escape an attack were well used to waiting until an attacking ship was overhead, when its ASDIC became of little use, and then altering course and increasing speed so as to get beyond the potentially damaging pattern of charges before it could explode. If that was successful, they knew that they then had twenty minutes or more before that ship could carry out another attack. It is difficult to imagine the horror of the first U-boat crew in finding that the charges were all around them before the ship had even caught up with them, and that was of great tactical use to the corvettes. Their successes would prevent the submarine crews from spreading the word that the old ways were no longer effective.

The Hedgehog

This weapon, called a Hedgehog, was a spigot mortar mounted just ahead of the bridge on what would usually be the gun deck for the second gun. The Flowers had a 4 in. gun on the forecastle deck, but where the B gun would have been was a large circle of twenty metal spikes, each about 10 in. long. They were set into a steel bed sloping up at the rear so that the spikes pointed forward at about thirty degrees from the vertical. These spikes were in a circle about 12 ft across and were the spigots onto which small mortar bombs were placed. When discharged, these bombs flew out ahead of the ship in a circle which gradually increased in diameter until they hit the water, at which point they began to sink in a circle about 100 ft across. The distance ahead of the ship at which the pattern entered the water was fixed at about 200 ft, and the timing of their release was decided either by the ASDIC installation or by the captain The ship's speed relative to the submarine was the deciding factor and that was best left to the automatic release capability.

These were relatively small charges, about 20 lb of Amatol, but if they were detonated around the submarine as intended they would be equivalent to a 'straddle' by two depth charges of 200 lb each. This would normally destroy much of the submarine's capability, if not rupture its hull.

Why was the Hedgehog not the Complete Answer?

Although their surprise effect was certain, their lethality was not guaranteed. The problem with these was that although the ship had ASDIC type 147, which gave the target submarine's depth, the mortar bombs only had two depth settings – namely shallow and deep. The choice of depth was set automatically just before firing, but neither setting was necessarily accurate, so far as the particular submarine under attack was concerned. The shallow setting was 90 ft and the deep setting 150 ft, and a submarine at halfway between those depths might well escape fatal damage, even if much equipment was destroyed or damaged. In that situation the captain might well decide to use the Hedgehog and then go round quickly for a depth charge attack.

An advantage of this relatively light weapon was that many reloads could be carried and a second attack could be launched within about six minutes of the first and that interval was well within the time that a second attack might become feasible by going round again. The other factor was that, with proper ship handling following the launch of the missiles, the ASDIC need never lose the submarine as it inevitably did with a depth charge attack, and so a second attack was nearly always possible within a short time. This was made even more likely because the Flower Class could turn very sharply compared with the much longer destroyer hull.

These various factors made the Flowers very able escorts at a critical time in the Battle of the Atlantic and there were a lot of them being built at small yards all around the country. That was possible because their single screw was driven by a triple expansion steam engine with a standard boiler. They had no gearbox and nothing very different, apart from the armament and sensors, from the hundreds of small merchant ships which had been built for many years and were familiar to the draughtsmen and tradesmen in the shipyards involved. With one destroyer and five corvettes a standard convoy was relatively better protected in 1943 than at any time in the war.

What Next?

In late 1942, another class of corvettes was in production – the Castle Class. Apart from its armaments, the major difference between the Flowers and the Castles was that the latter were very largely prefabricated at sites remote from the building yards and assembled on the launching ways in a relatively short time. Whole sections of the hull, complete with pipe work and electric cabling, furniture and ventilation trunking, were brought on vast trailers to the launching ways and welded together so that the ship could be launched within days rather than weeks and the fitting-out completed once it was afloat in the usual way; again, much more quickly because of the prefabrication. Six weeks from start to final trials was sometimes achieved.

The Castles were slightly, longer and slightly faster than the Flowers, but the major advance for anti-submarine action was the new mortar. Like the Hedgehog, it was mounted on the second gun deck just ahead of the bridge but, unlike the earlier mortar, this one was a highly sophisticated and manoeuvrable weapon. It was called the Squid mortar.

The Squid Mortar

This weapon benefited from all the many lessons learnt about beating the U-boat, and it had many advances in hardware as a result. First and foremost it was a three-barrelled device with the barrels mounted on a fore and aft axis in a stout base. The barrels were slightly offset from each other on the axis so that the three bombs, when launched, would form a triangle with about 50 ft sides on entering the water ahead of the ship. Furthermore, the axis was not only stabilised against the roll of the ship by being powered by an electric motor and remotely controlled from a gyroscope within the bridge structure, but the barrels could also be trained so that the point of impact in the water could be adjusted for the relative positions of the ship and the submarine. The ship no longer needed to be aimed at the submarine because the Squid mortar could be independently aimed within an arc of about twenty degrees either side of the bow.

The three bombs were fused for depth as a group so that one would be slightly above, one slightly below and one on the set depth and, with ASDIC 147 to give the depth of the submarine, the bombs could now be set very accurately to explode around the target, again by remote control right up to the moment of launch. Their charge was 100 lb of Amatol and they were thus a very powerful weapon, even compared with the depth charge, because of their greater accuracy and their coordinated depth settings. Once again, reloading could be achieved in minutes from nearby stowages and many more bombs could be stowed in the enlarged magazine below decks. This vessel was the very best anti-submarine escort ever to be commissioned in World War Two. However, its late arrival meant that, of the sixty ships ordered, only thirty-one were commissioned as fighting ships before the end of the attacks on convoys. Of the remainder, those already laid down were completed as general purpose hulls for a variety of uses but the rest were cancelled.

General Advances in Warfare at Sea

The developments described above, peculiar to anti-submarine activity, were confined to specialised ships such as corvettes, but there were other advances in hardware and tactics which applied to all warships.

There were two principal changes, the first being the introduction of short-range voice radio so that ships and aircraft could communicate rapidly by speech rather than by Morse code using lights or radio, or by signal flags. The second modification was the general fitting of Radio Direction Finding (RDF) which came to be known as radar, just as ASDIC became known as sonar once the American and British fleets began to operate together regularly following the attack on Pearl Harbour.

There were two main variants of radar: the general surveillance type, which had a continuously rotating aerial thus giving a plan picture of the surrounding sea and air, and a fixed radar used with gunnery systems and which was confined to providing range and bearing data on a selected target. With this latter type, the aerial was trained round onto the bearing of the target (and elevated onto an aircraft target where the gunnery system was for anti-aircraft use).

For corvettes the surveillance radar was the significant one and this allowed the operator to examine the sea's surface for 10 to 12 miles around the ship, or even further in ideal conditions. The ship's operations room, therefore, had available a plan view of all the convoy as well as the escorts and could safely manoeuvre at high speed at night or in poor visibility as well as in daylight.

Anti-submarine Radar

Those who saw the film *The Cruel Sea* will recall that the *Compass Rose*, a Flower Class corvette, had been abandoned, stationary astern of the convoy, in order to repair a propeller shaft defect. On completion of the repair, she then set off to catch up with the main body and detected a submarine ahead of her on the surface which was tracking the convoy in daylight in preparation for a night attack. This detection was at about 10 miles and was on a submarine conning tower in relatively calm sea. Had the weather been bad, with high winds and breaking waves, the range of detection could well have been less than 4 miles and only then by an experienced operator, but the radar was a threat to submarines on the surface at night as well as by day and this restricted their ability to concentrate against a convoy by running on the surface at the speeds of up to 20 kt attainable by the latest U-boats. There was also the additional threat that a submarine periscope could be detected at night as well as by day in a calm sea. Periscope watch had always been a daylight task for lookouts in all the ships of the convoy but the ability to detect them in poor visibility, and at night, was a further advance.

This was not a certainty however; a periscope not moving through the water is a very small target and in good weather the submarine captain, with his boat at rest, needed to show only 10 or 12 in. of the periscope for a few seconds in order to check his target position or to look all round for possible attackers. A very smart operator might catch him but could never be certain. If, however, the submarine was under way and the periscope was throwing up a small wash, this would register on the radar scope as a much larger blip. In ideal conditions such a blip might be observed by an astute operator at about a 2-mile range on a radar set operating on a 10 cm wavelength which was then the standard for small ships.

What About Developments in the U-boats?

There were several major developments which affected the ability of surface ships to detect and attack a U-boat. The ability of the target to hear sonar transmissions had improved significantly and the underwater speeds had been increased from below 8 kt to as much as 18 kt while the speeds on the surface were now close to 30 kt for the latest larger boats with increased horsepower. The snorkel, the breathing tube which allowed submarines to operate on diesel engines while submerged, was not a significant factor because few boats were fitted with them unless they had been built during late 1944. In any case, the snorkel was of most use when a boat was on passage to and from its base where previously an attack by aircraft could prevent a surfaced submarine from reaching its operating area or delay it significantly by forcing it to submerge. Once in its area, there would be little advantage in using the snorkel when in the vicinity of an escort because the very large wash and the plume produced by the snort mast could be detected by radar.

Their increased speeds did not seriously diminish the corvette's ability to engage them once they were in contact by sonar, and the higher speeds meant that the U-boats could be heard using passive devices as well as detected by searching sonar beams. It was unlikely that an attacking submarine would use its high speed except to get away from an attacker, and the ability of the Squid mortar to follow a change of bearing was significant in that situation.

Conclusion

Altogether, the 1943 summer saw a very sharp defeat for the U-boats and paved the way for some very successful convoy operations with large bodies of troops and many tons of equipment reaching the UK for the build-up to the invasion of France. It also permitted the confident plans to invade North Africa direct from the USA.

The turn round came about because the shipyards, workshops and aircraft factories in the UK were able to build, and get operational, a vast number of specialised aircraft, anti-submarine ships and weapons at a time when resources and raw materials were stretched in every direction, and when manpower was under many threats such as a low-protein diet, rationing of many essentials, blackouts, bombing and family disruption. While the sustained bravery and dedication to duty of those serving in the forces on land, in the air and at sea were well known and well recognised, there were no medals just for 'getting on with the job' and this is what I want to address in this account of the Battle of the Atlantic.

HMS Firedrake

This escort was one of eight of the *Fearless Class* built in the 1930s, being commisioned in 1932. She was 318 ft long and displaced 1375 tonnes, mounting four 4.7 in guns, one 3 in anti-aircraft gun and six smaller guns such as multiple pompoms. The main armament was four 21 in torpedo tubes with reloads. She was driven at 36 kt by two geared turbines.

Note that the mast is almost entirely clear of radio aerials and that there are depth charge rails visible at the stern and the shadow of one thrower on the port side aft.

HMS Afridi (H79)

She was one of sixteen Tribal Class fleet destroyers built in the late 1930s being commissioned in 1937. She was 350 ft long and displaced 1870 tonnes. She had six 4.7 in guns in three twin mountings, one twin 4 in anti-aircraft gun and seven smaller guns. The main armament was four 21 in torpedo tubes with reloads. She was driven by two geared turbines at 35 kt.

Once again the masts are almost without radio aerials and depth charge rails can be seen at the stern. No throwers appear to be fitted.

HMS Clarkia (K88)

The Flower Class corvettes were one of the most successful convoy escorts. They were built from 1940 to 1943 – eighty in Scotland and England, eight in Canada and eighteen in the USA – and subsequently transferred to the RN under Lend-Lease. Clarkia was built at Harland and Wolff and commissioned in 1940 and was thus without radar. They were 200 ft long and displaced 925 tonnes. The single 4 in gun was mounted forward and there was a pompom and several 20 mm guns for air defence, but the main armament was anti-submarine and consisted of depth charge rails and throwers. The ahead-throwing Hedgehog spigot mortar is just ahead of the bridge structure. They were driven at 16 kt by a single triple expansion steam engine.

HMS Berkley Castle (H378)

The Castle Class would no doubt have outshone the Flower Class had the Battle of the Atlantic continued into 1945; sixty-two were ordered and building began in early 1943 but only thirty-one had been commissioned by the end of 1944. The remainder already laid down were completed for a variety of other purposes; any not laid down were cancelled. They were slightly longer than the Flower Class and displaced 1010 tonnes. They had a single 4 in gun and several 20 mm for air defence. As with the Flowers, their main armament were depth charges on rails and throwers plus a much improved ahead-throwing weapon, the Squid mortar, which can be seen under its canvas cover just ahead of the bridge structure. They were slightly faster at   18 kt but were again driven by a single triple expansion steam engine.

The radar 271 scanner in its lantern (the scanner itself was not waterproof) and the huff-duff aerial at the top of the mast are clearly visible.

Getting the Ships to Sea

This section is an account of my personal experiences in ship-building in Sunderland, a small town on the river Wear which had for centuries built small ships for the coal trade and merchant ships of up to 4000 tonnes. The narrow river made the launching ways of limited length and so the size of ships was similarly limited. Nevertheless, while the river Tyne built larger ships, many of them, such as cruisers and aircraft carriers for the Royal Navy, the river Wear consistently sent greater total tonnage to sea throughout the months and years of the Second World War.

Why go to Sunderland?

When the war began in September 1939 I was a happy student apprentice working for Marryat and Place, a major electrical installation contractor in London. Apprentices were sent out to work with tradesmen for eight-week stints and then sent to Northampton Polytechnic (now the City of London University) for four weeks of lectures to study for the Higher National Certificate in Electrical Engineering. But within one year it would all have collapsed and I would be in Sunderland, working for the Sunderland Forge and Engineering Company.

Things began to change one weekend in June 1940 when I was spending some time at home with my parents in Folkestone, Kent. We had just finished breakfast when an aircraft droned in from seaward and dropped a bomb 100 yds away, demolishing two houses and rattling all our windows. That same weekend, ships began to arrive in the harbour laden with exhausted men rescued from the beaches around Dunkirk. As I took the train back to London on the Sunday evening we were held up in many wayside stations waiting for special trains to unload their cargoes of soldiers who were met by the Women's Voluntary Service (WVS) with tea and sandwiches, before being dispersed to tented camps. I got to work all right on the Monday but things had only just begun to get difficult.

At that time my father was running his Electrical Contractors business in Folkestone and in July he was told that all unessential businesses in the 'defence area' being established opposite the French coast were to be shut down and their owners and staff sent elsewhere. So, at forty-five years of age, my father was out of work and he and my mother were homeless as their cliff-top house had been taken over by the army.

I heard about all this by letter while I was working on a large laboratory installation for the Air Ministry Test House in Hertfordshire, about forty miles out of London where I lodged with the village constable in Harefield. Because my father was a nationally well-known electrical engineer with many acquaintances in the profession, and because he had served in the Royal Engineers in the First World War, he was quickly offered a job at Sunderland Technical College to teach the recruits of the newly formed Royal Electrical and Mechanical Engineers. He and my mother moved with what they could carry to a flat in The Elms in Sunderland, leaving all their other possessions in boxes with friends and relatives and their house to the mercy of the Royal Artillery.

I sympathised greatly and was able to assure them that with my lodging allowances and weekly pay I could support myself for the time being, at least until the Technical College courses I was doing in London restarted in September, when my wages and allowances would all stop for four weeks while I was attending college with the other apprentices in my year.

For a week or two things were fairly stable, but then the bombing of London began. The first effect was that the Northampton Polytechnic College opening was delayed and eventually the courses we were doing were cancelled until further notice. That was very good news for me because my financial independence could continue, uninterrupted by college attendance.

Then I received a telephone message from the firm's head office telling me that my London lodging had been demolished and that I should visit to salvage what I could. I borrowed a bicycle and went east, along the Great West Road, to reach Tottenham Court Road where I had lived for two years in a rented room at the Young Men's Christian Association. There was little left of the building and all I could find was my large wooden T-square and a rather torn dressing gown; they had survived because they had been hanging behind the door. All the rest was under tons of rubble.

I begged a bed for the night from a friend and the next day went to the Marryat and Place's company office in the City to speak with the apprentice supervisor, Mr John Marryat. I then went back to my lodgings, forty miles out, where I worked and began an exchange of letters with my parents.

I Migrate Too…

First and foremost, the apprentice supervisor had stated that the courses in electrical engineering would not restart and that they could no longer guarantee an education for their apprentices. Furthermore, they told me that I would soon be moved to other work back in the City and would therefore need somewhere to live when I left my temporary lodging in Harefield. The upshot was that my father confirmed that I could continue to work for my Higher National Certificate at the Technical College in Sunderland and that the many firms around there were crying out for electricians – I could easily find a job.

To me there seemed to be no real alternative; nobody could foresee the cessation of the Nazi bombing campaign, I could not find and pay for another lodging in London where homeless people were filling all the available rooms, and any hopes I had of getting qualified as a professional engineer, which was the point of my original apprenticeship, now seemed remote unless I moved.

I again visited the company office in the City and received back my endorsed indenture stating that I had completed half of my apprenticeship successfully, and took my leave of the many friends that I had made in the three years that I had worked there. I also visited the polytechnic and got my National Certificate course documents to prove my educational status after two years of the three-year course. Then I took the train from King's Cross, carrying my small suitcase and my toolbox, all that I now possessed in the world.

Arriving in Sunderland

My father met me at Newcastle Station on one late September afternoon and we travelled the twenty miles to Sunderland together on the local train. It was the first time we had been face-to-face since the previous June, when they had left Folkestone amid much general social confusion and total family disruption. In that interval our relationship had changed a lot; I had become financially independent and had started to take charge of my own life and to make my own decisions – not a very precocious condition for a nineteen-year-old, but a complete change for me. After forty minutes of cautious discussion about the past, we emerged from the station onto Fore Street and took a tram to the flat where my parents were living.

It was a top-floor flat with a staircase to the unused attic rooms; I noticed a small room on the half landing which had a small round window looking south, out onto the surrounding grounds. It could easily take a single bed and some shelves for my few possessions and appealed to me far more than the attic which was lofty and dusty with no view from the skylights. So I moved into that small room, slept on the floor and lived out of my suitcase for the first week until I got the shelves and hooks organised for some hangers and they had bought a single bed. There was plenty of spare bedding in the large linen cupboard and it was quite snug; I fixed a reading lamp from a socket on the landing and felt quite at home.

I found my way about in the first few days. My father went to the Technical College daily by tram and my mother and I went to look at the river Wear which divided the town, and we visited the sea at Seaburn and the few shops in the streets which appeared very dingy to us.

My most important task now was to find work, and I began by visiting the labour exchange. It was there that my struggles with the language began. It was not a matter of different words being used, but different usages of the familiar words which confused me. There was also the pronunciation problem: the people that I spoke to were educated, but their speech was a cross between what I seemed to recognise as Scottish vowels and a variety of consonants which received an added letter 'y' after them. It became familiar after a month or two but to begin with it made conversation tricky. My Kent speech was described as 'cockney', and that hurt to begin with.

The clerk at the labour exchange asked me where I had come from and what I had been doing.

'Were ye an apprentice?'

'Did ye finish ye time?'

'Why were ye sacked?'

It went on for some time but eventually we established what had happened and they accepted the evidence of my endorsed indenture and my 'cards' which showed me as fully paid-up in all respects.

'Ye can be employed as an apprentice by any firm which agrees to take ye on but not as an improver or a tradesman. Now what is ye trade?'

'I am an electrical fitter.'

'Can ye use a micrometer?'

'Yes.'

'Can ye use a lathe?'

'Yes.'

'Then ye are a fitter.'

I explained that I was an electrician who happened to be able to use a lathe and other metalworking tools.

'Can ye wire up an electric motor?'

'Yes.'

'What size of motor?'

'The largest I have dealt with alone was a hundred horse-power.'

'Can ye do conduit work and sheathed cable systems and connect them up?'

'Yes.'

'Then ye are an electrician.'

I pointed out that my indenture stated that I had studied for both the Electrical and the Mechanical National Certificates and City and Guilds Grade Two in electrical engineering.

The papers were taken away for consultation behind a glass screen. When the clerk returned she brought a supervisor along who said, 'You can be employed either as a fitter or as an electrician, but we cannot approve you for both on our books. Now what is it to be?'

So by the stroke of a pen I became an electrician. I was given a card which stated that I was allowed to seek work and that I was to come to meet the employment officer in a week's time. The supervisor was very helpful and gave me the address of a firm who had advertised vacancies for electricians and who might well take an apprentice.

Finding Work

The man who interviewed me at the firm involved was certainly willing and, after a few questions, he offered me a job at a large site at Spennymoor.

'There is a bus for our men going both ways and ye'll be paid for the travelling time.'

I asked what time we would be back in Sunderland, explaining that I was starting evening classes that week at Sunderland Technical College which began at seven-thirty in the evening.

'Ye would not be back before eight at neet but ye get meal allowances and overtime for that.'

He clearly thought that he had a winning hand, but I explained why I could not accept because I had an unfinished course with a year to run. I said that I would come back if I could not do better.

'Sorry lad, that is the job that we have and ye moost tak it or leave it. I shall be sorry if ye leave it.'

I went away feeling sorry too, it had sounded like a good job with a good employer but my mind was set on achieving the Higher National Certificate if at all possible, and I felt that I had something to offer to an employer who would give me time off. However, when I went back to the labour exchange the supervisor did not like me one little bit; he obviously felt that I should be getting on with proper work and not fiddling around with school at my age. I was sent away and again told to come back in a week's time; this time I was given no addresses.

Meanwhile my father had been told by a colleague that the Sunderland Forge and Engineering Company had several sponsored students at the Tech and that they were always looking for electricians. He suggested that I try the Sunderland Forge and he had the name of the manager, Mr Gurney. I looked up their address and it was in Pallion so I got a tram most of the way and just walked into the main office and asked to see Mr Gurney.

'Have ye an appointment?'

'No, but I have been told that he needs qualified electricians and I am looking for a job.'

After a short wait I was taken upstairs and ushered into the office of a fierce-looking man – Mr Gurney. I later learned that he was known as 'the Big Fella' and was the outside manager of electricians. He was distinguished from 'the Quair Fella' who was the outside foreman, Mr Wrightson. The Big Fella grilled me very thoroughly about my work in London; he already knew of Marryats, my London employer, because a subsidiary of Marryats called Dewhurst and Partner made control equipment for some of their winches. I had known about Sunderland Forge cranes and winches and had worked on some in London docks but had not, until then, connected the two in my mind.

He seemed satisfied and agreed that if I worked satisfactorily for them until I was twenty-one then he would be prepared to endorse my indenture which I had shown to him. He was also sympathetic to my wish to continue my studies for a Higher National Certificate and said, 'I know that Mr Wrightson will support you but he cannot tell any chargeman how to run his job and to give you time off. A chargehand may be willing to treat you differently but all our jobs are undermanned and they are working overtime most nights of the week and all the weekends to finish the jobs. Don't come running to me if you get opposition from some marker-off or chargeman; you must come to some agreement with them about it yourself.'

I did not entirely understand what he was telling me but it sounded all right, if a bit more complicated that I had expected.

'Have you ever worked on ships?'

The idea had never entered my head; I had assumed doing some shop work to be followed by installation of winches and cranes somewhere and I told him so, and why.

'You may well work on winches but if you do, it will be aboard a steamer. All our work is on ship installations anywhere from here to Blyth Dock, Middlesbrough and the Tyne. We do tramps, colliers, tankers and naval ships of all kinds including aircraft carriers in the larger yards on the Tyne. I will ask Mr Wrightson to see that you work in a Sunderland Yard so that you can get to your night classes. They are all getting on with their work and we are still talking. Now do you want the job?'

I did and I said that I could start as soon as the paperwork was done at the labour exchange where they were expecting me at the end of the week. He said that all that would be done in their office, and then he made an internal telephone call.

'Mr Wrightson is in his office and will see you now. Good luck and I will see you again when you have your National Certificate.'

I went down the stairs to meet the Quair Fella and found a very different man from Gurney. He was much gentler, tired-looking and wore a filthy raincoat and a battered felt hat; his glasses were cracked and mended with electrician's tape.

He gave me a short questioning and said, 'Weel ye'll find ships different from lifts and factories but ye have a guid background and all ye need to dee is keep ye wits aboot yer and to get along wi' the lads.

'Now, tak a car to Wearmouth Bridge and get off afore it gans ower to Fore Street. On the south side ye will see a slope leading doon te Austin's Shipyard; gan doon ther. They build colliers and tramps and we have a team ther arl the year. The chargeman is Bobby Potts. Ask for him at the gyate and say ye are from the Forge and they'll tell ye wher to gan. He'll be on 481, at Number Two slip I expect. Bobby's ahlreet and if ye've any sense ye'll be OK ther.'

His language was Wearside, one version of the Geordie talk, close to Scots but with those odd vowels and the altered initial consonants that I would come to know well. It was now twelve o'clock and I went home for lunch and told my mother what was happening. She was not as pleased as I was.

'I have been here three months now and I know what a rough lot these shipyard men are. They are dirty and foul-mouthed and they speak an abominable cant called Wearside. If I ever hear you talking like that it will break my heart.'

I remembered that she was unaware of some of the roughneck men at Marryats; Bert Veck whom I had worked with for several months had an awesome collection of oaths, some in Hindustani, which he had taught me, so I did not worry unduly about her concerns. I had survived worse things than foul talk.

After lunch, I put on my overalls, picked up my tool bag and took the tram to the bridge as directed; I had been across it before but not with a view to working there and I now saw that below the bridge there was a large fitting-out yard with a floating dock and a dry dock, as well as the quay at which a rusty hull was lying. A sign painted in large white letters on the main building read: AUSTINS AND SONS, SHIP BUILDERS AND REPAIRERS. The whole area was wreathed in smoke and although it was 80 ft below me the noise was deafening. As I walked down the slope I could see further round the bend of the river where there were several launching ways. A guard at the gate wore a quasi police uniform and a leather belt with a holster. I don't know if there was a weapon in it and I never asked.

'I am looking for the Sunderland Forge chargeman, please. His name is Bobby Potts.'

'Oh, aye, oor Robbie. He's on 481 at Number One quay. I expect his store is in the forepeak, it usually is. What's yer nyam?'

I told him my name was Tommy Gilbert; it was a flash of cowardice, but I could not somehow see the name Martin finding much conviction in such surroundings. I walked through the yard which was crowded with stacks of steel plates, bags of rivets and many piles of shaped steel bars. Any clear ways were also occupied by railway lines and there was a shunting process going on near to the jetty. I found myself at the foot of a steep wooden gangway and climbed to the top where a man, wearing a cap with a shiny peak, sat smoking a short pipe.

'Is this 481?' I asked him.

'Why, aye, madder. Whe de ye want te see?'

'Bobby Potts, please.'

'Up the forepeak madder.'

He pointed, and although this was the first ship apart from cross-Channel ferries that I had ever boarded, I walked towards what I had noted as the sharp end, past a raised superstructure and then down a steep iron ladder, past two cargo holds and at the end of that there was a raised forecastle with two doors, one on each side of the fore hold. In the door on my side there was a chap in brown overalls with a cap and he was watching me as I came towards him.

'Are you Mr Potts?'

'I yam that. Whe are ye?'

I saw that he had no teeth at all.

'I'm an apprentice electrician. My name is Tommy Gilbert and Mr Wrightson sent me down to work here.'

He stepped back into the wardrobe-sized space which was fitted out with rough wooden shelves and a small sloping one used as a desk. He turned his head and spoke to some invisible person.

'Fetch Shortarse oop hyere and tell him I've got a cockney myat fer him.'

A little rabbity man scuttled past us and went out down the deck.

When, a few months later, I told Bob that my name was really Martin, he hooted, 'When I saw ye wi ye little bag like a candy-man coomin doon the deck and then ye telt me ye wore working fer me; if ye'd telt me ye nyam was Mairt'n, I'd have pissed mesel. Ye dyoon reet man, Tommy is better.'

A candyman was a junk dealer who went from door to door asking for second-hand stuff and offered other tawdry goods like soap and cheap perfume in exchange; it was not thought to be a man's work in Sunderland.

'Shortarse' turned out to be a sandy-haired lad whose name was Longbottom; I later found out that he was in his final year as an apprentice and was working alone as a tradesman. At that time he was the only one with Bob because the ship had been launched just that morning and electrician's work was just beginning, so I would see the whole thing through from start to finish. He took me aft along the deck and up to the superstructure, which was a rusty edifice about three decks high with a few large rectangular holes cut here and there to give access and light within. One opening at upper deck level led into a large open area which he called the saloon. As time went on this space which stretched the full width of the ship would be divided by wooden bulkheads to form the officers' mess, several cabins and a pantry. There were four or five men working there with saws and chisels putting up these thick plywood bulkheads. I saw that there were lead-sheathed cables clipped to strips of wood running here and there overhead and where there were bulkheads the cables ran down to what were obviously switch positions.

'Weel, Tommy man, here's where we are working the noo. The lighting is single pole switches and you can put them on for me. There are wooden blocks in that bag and switches in that box. Can ye dee that ahlreet?'

I said that I could and noted that there were cables already identified at each switch position in the standard manner which City and Guilds courses prescribed; that at least was unchanged with the higher latitude. I took a teak block and a standard Crabtree switch and marked the necessary holes on the block and a fixing hole in the centre, plus a slot at the side to allow the cables to be entered behind the block. I had done it hundreds of times and worked swiftly. Then I got out my carpenter's brace and a ¼ in. bit and began to drill the block as usual. To do this I had placed it on a standard sawing horse which was standing nearby.

'Get away from that stool ye booger.'

I noticed that I was the centre of a ring of men glaring at me. Shortarse approached and bleated.

'Eh man Tommy, them blocks is joiner's work. Gie it te the joiner te cut and drill.'

I explained that I had always cut and drilled my own blocks in London and they said in chorus, 'Ye can keep ye cockney ways oot o' this yard or we'll ahll be oot reet away.'

I apologised and asked who would do the work. A young joiner stuck his hand out.

'Ah dee the electrician's work. Gie us them here.'

I handed over the three that I had marked and waited for him to do them. Meanwhile, I thought about this hard division of skills and realised that for some of them this was the first regular work for more than ten years following the depression, and that trade differences were always aggravated by years of shortage of work. Every man guarded his trade fiercely and I was reminded of barristers and solicitors, of GPs and consultant surgeons and many other professions which had similar rules of precedence and areas of responsibility.

Bobby laughed out loud showing all his toothless gums when

Shortarse told him about it at three o'clock. This was the traditional break for our tea made by Sid, the rabbity labourer. I later found that he was also a bookie's runner and he helped me to win a few shillings as time went on and I got to know him better.

'Well, ye've myad yer mark man, Tom.'

I had indeed. My trespass soon spread round the yard and became Forge folklore within a very few days and would be quoted to me for months to come as evidence of cockney stupidity. It was all very friendly with them, but in the saloon on that first day there had been nothing friendly about it at all.

Another man joined later in the week, but to begin with there were just the three of us and I spent a lot of time simply finding my way about the ship: the cavernous boiler room and engine room, empty as yet, the tiller flat where the steering gear would be installed and the stokehold with odd names such as 'the fiddly top' for the steel grating above the stokehold. I already knew about the forepeak and the tiller flat but there was plenty more to learn. The ship was a standard collier design: two holds forward with a mast between them, then the bridge superstructure and two more holds with a mast between them aft of the bridge and right aft the crew's accommodation. They were being built in their scores up and down the coast and were used for transporting coal from the many Durham pits down to the power stations and gas works in the south from London to Shoreham. These seaways were wide open to attack by aircraft and E-boats and the East Coast Convoys were regularly sought by the enemy from the outbreak of the war. They formed a vital lifeline, and replacing sunken ships and repairing damaged ones was our work. Our shipyard was expected to complete one new ship every ten or twelve weeks and to cope with damaged ships as they arrived.

The standard collier's displacement was about 5000 tonnes and the installation of the engines and boilers would take place elsewhere because Austins had no engine capability and subcontracted that part of the job, as they did their electrical installation work. The engine contractor would fit a triple expansion steam engine, driving the screw directly and there would be two water tube boilers connected to a single funnel which would pass up through the after accommodation. It had not changed much in a hundred years and everyone knew exactly how it was to be done and so men were fleeted from ship to ship as needed: platers and riveters first, then joiners and electricians, followed by engine fitters and finally by the painters and upholsterers.

There was another hull already rising on slipway Number Two recently vacated by 481. Although Kaiser may have revolutionised shipbuilding on the green field sites in the USA, here, with our limited space and narrow rivers, there was not much scope for change. However, we worked until 9 p.m. every night except Saturday and Sunday to expedite completion of these vital ships. Saturday afternoon was sacred to football at Roker Park, but Sunday work was just 8 a.m. to 5 p.m. On Sunday there was one hour for lunch, but on the other days it was one and a half hours, with half an hour for tea. It all made for a very full week.

On arrival in Sunderland I had signed on at the Technical College for the National Certificate course final year without difficulty, having brought my session exam paper results with me. The classes started at 7.30 p.m. and went on until 9 p.m. on Mondays, Tuesdays and Wednesdays and I had already attended for two weeks from the start of their autumn term in October. I asked Bob in my first week about getting time off for them and he agreed without any hesitation.

'I wish I had dyon it mesel Tommy. Some apprentices did and they are ahl deein' better than me. When de ye tak yer exam, Tommy man?'

I explained that I hoped to take the national final in April 1941 and if successful I could then sign on for the Higher National Certificate and take that exam in April 1943.

'Ad away man. Ye'll be working for bluidy Hitler be then.'

He understood what I was doing and why, but he said that he expected me to be extra diligent in return so that the other men on the job would not see me as skiving at their expense. I knew that I would need to spend at least four hours at weekends on homework and with my long shipyard hours as well my future would be one long slog, no skiving about it as I told him. For myself, I knew that I was young and fit, I would soon know my job in ships backwards and I was confident that I could do the technical work in the evenings without undue stress. I decided that I should do my homework on Sunday evenings but to indulge in some relaxation on Saturday nights. I was influenced because the lads always talked about their Saturdays when they used to meet in town for a beer. I knew that I would have more arguments with my mother about that but would face it when it came.

I had probably worked as hard in London when doing both day and evening classes and working all over the place with long travelling time on some days. I was now living at home which made it all a lot easier because I no longer needed to be self-catering as well as hard working. Regarding my future at 'the Forge', I knew that I could satisfy Bob or any other charge hand where my standard of work was concerned. The team on the ship built up to fourteen including seven tradesmen and four more apprentices, and, as I got to know them over the weeks leading up to Christmas, I realised that although they all knew much more about ships and things seagoing than I did, knowledge which they shared with me at every opportunity, I could leave most of them behind on the technicalities of electrical work. This was not an opinionated attitude, they were all capable of it but had no family expectation that they would qualify technically and no encouragement from their employer to start further education. The Forge did employ about six student apprentices and they were working at day classes for the Higher National Diploma which was technically equivalent to an engineering degree. All of them had qualified by matriculating at the grammar school but I was too old to join them as I later found when talking again to Mr Gurney.

Wearside People, 1941

I cannot remember where I first heard of Geordie Teignmouth, but I recall registering his name one Saturday evening in the Queen's Bar.

'Aye he's a quair'un is Geordie. A bad booger, Tom, you don't wan get mixed oop wi him man.'

'Where does he work Bob?'

'Mostly up the Tyne man, Tom, admirality work's where he's usually been, on cruisers and the like but he was an apprentice with me for a while.'

'Well what's queer about him?'

'He's ower ready wi his fists, Tom, it's got worse since he knocked that teart's hip oot but he was always bad that way. He didna marry her but it narks him tha kna's and naebody dare mention it for fear he'll brae'em. He can too – he's a strong booger for ahl he's sae thin.'

I remembered all this one day in March when Geordie turned up at Austins yard to work on a job which Bob was just beginning there; it was what was called a 'flatiron ship'. These were especially low built colliers which were intended to go right up the River Thames to Battersea Power Station and to various gas works bordering the Thames above the many low bridges. They needed to withstand the rigours of the North Sea in winter so they were robust, and their hulls were of almost the usual form though without high forecastles; their superstructure was either very low or it was collapsible. The bridge structure was kept very low but the masts and funnels could be laid down flat when required. This particular version was an entirely new design with additional features such as power operated hatches over the four holds and power operated masts and funnel lowering; these facilities allowed for a smaller crew and reduced accommodation space. These extra facilities were all electrically powered and so the generating capacity was large for a ship of about 4000 tonnes.

Also, the main engines were diesels to remove the need for a boiler room with a large diameter funnel, merely an exhaust stack with air supply vents for the two big engines required.

She had novel armament too; we were talking to one of the draughtsmen about the communications to the gunnery platform and he said, 'There's summat new there an ahl but we have nae details so I canna tell ye whats wanted yit.'

'What is this she has then, Madder?' asked the driller.

'Its sommat called an Early Gun, very powerful they say.'

It was the first that we had heard of the Twin Oerlikon 20 mm cannon which was to revolutionise the air defence of these small ships from then on. Instead of a slow 12 pounder, plus two or three machine guns firing a solid 303 bullet, the Oerlikon sprayed out ninety rounds a minute of 20 mm explosive tracer shells which had a graze fuse and would take the wing off an aircraft if they struck. They were a lot better against both E-boats and aircraft and the DEMS gunners loved them. These were men of the Royal Artillery who had been allocated two per ship, and formed the crew of the Defensively Equipped Merchant Ships.

I was in charge of the engine room and generators as usual, Bob had given me a general run over the new requirements in the drawing office and then left me to work out the details on board, promising me another electrician, a labourer and a share of a driller and a welder when required. We had discussed with Mr Wrightson, the outside foreman, the best way of handling the comparatively heavy cables required by the enlarged generating capacity. It had been decided that the use of admiralty pattern, perforated steel trays would be better than our usual wooden strip or light-galvanised steel clips which might not properly bear the extra weight and could collapse when a bomb fell nearby; Bob said that he would get a man with experience of using admiralty metal tray. Geordie was that man, and he arrived in the empty engine room space one morning with his toolbox. I was surprised to be confronted by a dark, thin lad who was about my own age. He was bow-legged with long arms and taller than me by a head at least. Bob introduced us – me to him as 'that cockney lad ye'll have heard af.'

I asked this lad what he had heard and he said, 'If yer Tommy Gilbert they telt me tha kna's thi work.'

I had made a few tentative chalk marks around the place suggesting cable routes and positions for switchgear; these had been discussed with the plumber and the ships engineer. However, we could not decide quite how to route the large cables from the generator terminal boxes to their controlling switchboard and I mentioned this to Geordie.

'Eh, if it isna in't drawungs we'll find a way. Where ist the drawing man, Tom?'

I got out the positional drawings and circuit diagrams and there was no detail of fixing or anything else, just the cable sizes and destinations and some explanatory notes, figures and references to other drawings for pipes and other purely engineering details.

'Allus the way man, tells ye nowt,' he said, but was neither surprised nor downhearted.

'Can yer read all them circuits Tommy?'

I said that I could.

'Well ye tell me what's ther and Ah'l tell thee how to fix the cable runs.'

Some days later we had a well developed working partnership and the job went along nicely; at this stage we had a bare hull to work in and it was relatively simple to reeve and bend the large lead-sheathed cables in the confined space. It would have been much more difficult after the engines were installed because they dominated the low compartment.

It was before Easter so I was attending evening classes three nights a week and I was not sure how Geordie would react to this. He never once commented adversely on being left alone on three evenings each week (the labourer never did turn up) and we were able to agree what he needed to achieve before the next day or the next consultation. We did not move in the same circle of drinkers on a Saturday evening, although our paths crossed now and then as we went from bar to bar or to The Rink, the local dance hall.

We were talking one day about recreation as we worked and he said, 'One thing I like of a Sa'urday neet, Tom, an that's a bit o' the old root man.'

I did not understand exactly.

'The old leg ower, man.'

'How do you go about it then?'

'Why man I wer born in Sun'rland I ken ahl the girls, whe will and whe wilna. Ther's nowt int. But you need to watch the beer tha kna's; nae guid gett'n reet ther and then ye need the nettie. Eh I lost a few that way to begin with but na if Ah've me eye on a bit Ah drink whisky.'

'Where do you take them? A hotel?'

'Not likely, an hav everyyin tellin' mi Mam? Nae, doon bi the beach an ther's allus the park. Ye moos pick yer weather tha kna's. I'll show ye a few on 'em some neet if ye've a mind Tom?'

That was a very fair offer and I thanked him. I might even have taken him up had opportunity ever knocked but somehow the only time that I ever fell into Geordie's company, despite the months that we worked together in Austins, was one filthy rainy night when all that we did was sit in the Norfolk Bar where there was a piano and watch the pianist knocking out his regular repertoire. I sometimes played there at lunchtimes, but in the evenings nobody but the regular man was allowed on it for fear of damage or flooding with spilt beer. On this occasion we got quite merry and sang filthy songs to the piano; the publican did not complain and I heard later that Geordie had once blacked his eye for some chance insult and he now had no trouble in that pub. I never found Geordie anything other than pleasant, if rough-tongued company.

While I knew him there were other fights but he was not in any of them. I never heard that his partners in the 'leg ower' game were dissatisfied with whatever bargain they had; he was the only one of my acquaintances who took that particular sort of exercise regularly. The others, like me, were content to speculate about the girls, to talk about it over our beer but apart from the fairly frequent petting parties which grew out of somebody's birthday celebration there was little overt sex. We were all working hard, seven days a week. and I had, in addition, at least four hours homework every week during the winter months and that kept me at home on Sunday evenings – the traditional courting evening in Sunderland.

I know that whenever we needed the welder or the driller to help the job along a bit, it was Geordie who got it within the hour. Bob told me that he sometimes waited a day for a driller while Geordie had three or four holes drilled, for all that Bob was the chargeman. Geordie had charm and he was persuasive, so perhaps that is why the girls went for him.

I learnt to play dominoes (penny a knock) from Geordie at a nearby pub we used when eating our lunchtime sandwiches and it passed many a relaxing half-hour thereafter. Whenever I see a set of dominos now I am reminded of the violent smell of that pub where the publican was a cat lover with several of them resident. So far as I could judge they were all old males with weak bladder control. The beer was good though and with the windows open it was quite bearable.

The booze and the dance hall were the only pastimes available to apprentices once the weekly Saturday football game at Roker Park was over. I used to spend Saturday afternoon getting clean. A long bath while I scrubbed every part of my hands and arms, plus other parts where I could reach, seldom removed all of the week's grime. If I had been working while a ship was at the coal staithes, I would need to strip on returning home each evening, but even if I did so the weekly soak would not get rid of it all.

Once I had got reasonably clean, I would dress in my best and sort out my weekend's homework, ready for the Sunday night. I gave myself Saturday night off as the only real leisure that I could find in the winter; in summer there was more time because of the lack of evening classes and the light evenings after work. But in February and March 1941 the winter was hard, the wind constant and cold and the rain persistent and very wet.

My mother deeply deplored my 'plebeian' existence as she called it, but I liked the lads at work. I had absolutely nothing else to do and she could suggest nothing because Sunderland did not cater for intellectual pursuits in wartime; there was just no possibility that I would not relax at all from my heavy workload and so she put up with it. I was never in doubt about her feelings however.

On every Saturday I braved the weather to get down to one of the apprentices' favourite pubs, either the Queen's Hotel or the

Continental Hotel where five or six of us would be assembled by about eight o'clock and the evenings would develop from there. After work one day in August, in the bar at The Queen's Hotel, Bob said to me, 'The Quair Fella was here, Tom, and he's worried about ye an' Johnny Thorn fighting last Sa'urdee.'

'What the hell's it got to do with Wrightson what I do on my night off? It isn't as though we get all that much time to play.'

'It's not playin' that he's on about man, Tom, it's ye brayin' Johnny Thorn when he's half shot that Wrightson disna like.'

'He wasn't half shot, Bob, you know Johnny as well as I do and he can walk a chalk line with six pints in his guts. We had been drinking all the evening at The Sink and I was setting him home when he started talking about cockney bastards, so I gave him a couple of handsful. If he was half shot then the sly bugger must have been bumming scotch on the side.'

Bob called for a couple more pints of Vaux's bitter and paid Alice without comment to me. Then he said, 'Ye may have to talk to Wrightson bout it.'

I was still unused to such solicitude from any foreman.

'What has it got to do with him? I do my work, I never did a dud job for you and you know it – apart from that time we got the wrong drawings by mistake and you didn't blame me for that. Does he think the Forge has bought me?'

'It's not that, Tom,' said Bob patiently. 'He just disna like seeing two Forge apprentices making hexibitions round Fore Street. After ahl, ye worked four months with Johnny and you did some good work between ye, now it all seems sour.'

'I haven't worked with Johnny for weeks now and anyway, that honeymoon was over. Johnny didn't like me knocking off at five to go to night school; he said he was carrying the jobs while I was away.'

Bob was startled. 'Ah didna ken that man, Tom. Ah thowt better of him than that.'

'Oh it was all right on the Lambton boat. We worked in the engine room and did a better job than you expected. Eh Bob?'

'Ah'll admit that, Tom.'

'Then he got the marker-off's job at Thompson's and I went over there and worked with Big Bill for a couple of weeks and we didn't get in each other's way. But the next thing was that degaussing racket with the colliers overnight up at the staithes and we were on the go day and night for a week or two while we did several of them. It is no wonder we got on each other's nerves a bit. There's nothing in the job technically, it was plain boring, uncomfortable with all the teeming coal dust night after night – we did three in a row if you remember – and there we were, two good apprentices wasting our time technically and feeling their oats. You could have sent Spike up there or Harry and his dumb chum and they would have loved it.'

It was that second pint that had done it I suppose, that and the quick grog at dinner time in the corvette where the sailors had joined a week before; also I had not yet had any supper. Anyway I was letting off steam to Bob in a way which he had every right to resent as a chargeman dealing with one of his apprentices.

'I must go, Bob; my landlady will have my supper hot.'

'Aye lad, nae doot, but its not yer landlady calling I doubt its yer ould lady isn't it?'

'I suppose it is Bob, she gets home about now.'

'Where's she working these days, Tom?'

'She's with the soap people in Newcastle, Grainger Street or something like that.'

'Thomas Headleys is it?'

I remembered then and agreed that was the name of the firm.

'What dis she dae theer?'

I remembered my initial fury at Bob's personal questioning in the first week after my arrival when every remark brought a stream of questions which I, in my cockney ignorance, thought inquisitive and prying. I now knew that I must quench the indignation and accept the enquiries in the spirit that they were made – an invitation to friendship and intimacy of the kind offered by the Wearside men.

'She is a trained shorthand typist and secretary, Bob, and as she has been at the trade for many years she is some bigwig's personal assistant up there.'

'And wher er ye livin now man, Tom?'

'In Holmlands Park with a Mrs Milburn.'

The family had moved from The Elms flat when my father, as

a member of the Officers' Reserve, was called up and appointed Captain, Royal Engineers and so left his job at the Technical College to work as a garrison engineer in Thetford, Norfolk. Consequently, my mother then needed to work full time to support herself and my younger brother.

'Aye, I remember. Widow of a lawyer or the like,' said Bob.

Milburn was a solicitor who, when widowed, had employed her as his housekeeper and was now foster mother to his young son and daughter, and mother to his youngest child, another son who had escaped being posthumous by a few weeks when he died suddenly in 1940. Obviously such a local titbit of gossip would not have gone unnoticed by a fan of the *Sunderland Echo* like Bobby Potts. His glass was empty so I filled it again and paid Alice who gave me a nice little smile.

'What ye gan do Tom, yer nearly oot yer time?'

'Another year yet, Bob; nearly eighteen months before I get a man's pay.'

'Gan on man, yer deein a man's work noo.'

I was not so sure.

'I've been lucky Bob. I've always had a job that was child's play because of my experience in London and here I've been helped out by the lads when I was in trouble with the shop at Pallion. You gave me a fair crack right from the start but suppose I had started off with Willie?'

'Aye man, Tom, he'd have given ye a reet skelpin for yer funny talk an ahl.'

'When I went down to Greenwell's for a week or two after we finished the Lambtonian here he turned me over to McCluskey and said, "Here's some clever bugger of Potts'. See if he's any good. If Potts disna' want him he must be effin rubbish." What's more, I made a right balls of the first job he gave me and he sent me back to the shop two days later.'

Bob asked me what job it was.

'It was those hold signalling lights on the tanker conversion, the Bachaquero she was called. I wasn't the first to make a balls of it and it was due to that continuity man they had down there'.

'Yer mean oor Jackie?'

'That's him, a good tradesman no doubt but too keen on

making money quickly out of lumpers and to hell with the job.'

The next remark was a turning point if only I had known it; but these critical decisions have always crept up on me and I have long since learned to trust my intuition when faced with an unexpected but vital question.

'If ye want to get on better work I'd put in a word with Wrightson.'

This was a most generous gesture because I obviously made life easier for Bob by taking responsibility for the engine rooms and so on and he was offering to let me go elsewhere.

'Well, Bob, I would like to get onto those prefabricated frigates up at Pickersgill's if there's a chance.'

'But that's admirality work, man. Ye've never dyun any.'

'I have Bob, when Willie sent me back to the shop that time Wrightson sent me down to North Eastern Marine where there was a Flower Class corvette finishing. I was two weeks there with Stan and he put me on the ASDIC hut, when that was done I went on the Compass Correction system – that was something special. I got on well with Stan, he never cribbed about letting me off early for the evening classes although all the others worked on until nine every night.'

Bob knew why too.

'Why, aye, he went to neet schools hissel, got a certificate too; that's why he was the youngest chargeman at the Forge for years. When do you get your certificate, Tom?'

'I took the National Certificate last April and the results should be out soon. If I pass, I have another two years of classes until I take the Higher National in April 1943.'

'Tow year man? Ad away the invasion will be ahl ower and ye'll be slavin' for bloody Hitler.'

He was kidding, but I knew what he meant; the yards had a boom on their hands, having had starvation until 1937 and after. Any man who did not now make his £16 a week (£500 in today's money) by working every hour that was on offer while the sun was shining on the industry was a mug in his eyes. There was no difficulty about overtime; the problem was getting any time off. In winter, it was a relief to get to the college for three nights instead of shivering in a half-built ship with the temperature near freezing and a keen east wind blowing through every crevice of the unfinished structure. But in summer I was at it every night until 9 p.m., Saturday mornings and all day Sunday without any let-up. It was a real test of mental endurance unless I had something absorbing to do there, and that was why I wanted to get away from the simple little colliers which Bob had charge of.

So the word got to Wrightson that I would like to change to admiralty work; it was late summer before he sent for me.

'Ah'm gie'n ye a shift ti admirality work, Tom. Will ye gan ti Hawthorne Leslies the morn?'

That yard was on the Tyne and I knew from my mother's travel problems that I could not expect to return regularly for evening classes. I mentioned this to him, saying that I had a good chance of taking a Higher National in two years' time if I stuck to it.

'Ye want yer butter both sides then; ye can gan the morn or ye can stay with oor Robbie at Austins.'

I went back to see Bob before going home that evening and told him what had happened to his effort on my behalf. He just laughed and said, 'Dinnot worry man, he's just having' ye on.'

And so it was, a week later I was up at Pickersgill's working with Stan again.

Fun and Games

The apprentices' Saturday evenings were sacred to drink. The evening began with a few keen early starters sitting down between six and seven o'clock at some prearranged bar; others joined as time passed and by nine o'clock there was generally a feeling that a move was due.

Once the walking around began the course of the evening was determined by the weather or by the luck of a chance meeting with a rumour of good beer somewhere. By 1942, the standard draught beer became more and more like 'sugar alley watter', the politest description given to it, apart from George Youngers which was consistently good. If that was not available it had to be bottled beer, but this was very scarce too; to ensure a supply it was necessary to know the particular publican well and to book the bottles by the whole case before the evening began. This involved some determined shopping at preceding lunchtimes to 'set a case' for the mob on the coming Saturday. The most popular place with the group of apprentices that I worked with was known as 'The Sink'. This was the basement bar of the Continental Hotel and was presided over by Molly Heptinstall, a well-known and efficient barmaid who was rumoured to have a seaman on every collier trading out of Sunderland. She was the best barmaid that I have ever met from the drinker's point of view. If I whispered to her in her crowded bar at lunchtime on Friday, asking for two cases of Vaux's Double Maxim for us for the next night, she was always positive.

'Be hyere bi six thirty, Tommy, or they winna be kept.'

She knew well enough that if the lads started anywhere else she would lose their custom for that night at least. But even when we once arrived as late as eight o'clock, she had held back the precious bottles for us. I once cycled down to The Sink at lunchtime to fix two cases for that evening and ran into a birthday party – Molly's. So it was an hour and several whiskies later that I dragged myself away only to find that some bastard had pinched my bike.

The Saturday evenings were seldom alike, even when they began in a standard fashion; my recollection is of endless variants depending upon the places visited and the company encountered in the relatively limited area of Fore Street where the best pubs were. The Sunderland Forge apprentices numbered about thirty and they were as varied a collection of individuals as you would meet anywhere; their ages ranged from seventeen to twenty-one. After coming out of your time, you were expected to drink with the older men and leave the boys to make their own fun. There were the odd bachelors like Bobby Potts, who clung to their apprentice ways even after ten years of man's time, but they were few.

Within our very mixed group there were about twelve apprentices who could be relied upon to do a good job on the ship and who really understood what they were working with. This select team tended to remain together in the evenings while the others kept their own company. This happened apparently without any resentment although caustic remarks passed if two lots found themselves in the same bar. The parties generally met according to which chargeman they were with at the time because they could most easily arrange to meet but others would join as they happened to arrive. You might start in a school of four and later find that it had become ten with a sudden influx from some other bar. Occasionally it happened that one lad had a girlfriend that he had arranged to meet at a dance and then it was likely that the whole lot would agree to go too, (not always to give him support) and the girl might or might not appreciate the crowd. Equally, he might decide that he preferred the drink with his 'madders' and would give the girl a miss.

One or two nights stick out in my mind; we had agreed to meet at the Hat and Feather because Harry Heatley knew it as his local and said that the beer was good that week. So we had a few there and moved on to the Masons Arms where there was music from a piano accordion, and then on to The Sink for our treasured cases of Double Maxim. On this occasion there were six of us; Harry, Spike, Ginger, Reggie, Bobby Potts and me. We had two cases of pint bottles, forty-eight of them, and it was only 8.30 p.m. so we were doing nicely. There was a table for six in the middle but it was occupied and so we went to two smaller ones a little apart from each other. There were other seats around the walls and all were full, mostly older men, some with their wives. We called to Molly and she brought out the cases.

'Eh, Molly lass, Ah widna lak to wrestle wi thee,' said Ginger.

She dropped one on his foot and replied, 'Dinna fret Ginger, Ah doot oor lad ud let ye.'

Molly's brother, the 'lad' referred to, was a local copper and we had no doubt that he would 'not let' Ginger, meaning restrain him. But since Molly was not known to be on speaking terms with her brother that week, the joke was to decide whether she wanted it one way or the other – Ginger could not decide and worried over it all the evening.

Reggie Laithwaite was a suave young man, better dressed than most of us. We all spent money and clothing coupons on our 'best' but somehow Reggie always had the edge sartorially.

After about an hour doing justice to our stock of bottles and talking about everything under the sun Reggie said, 'Away up The Barns the noo lads. I telt oor lass Ah'd see her there.'

'Yer Mam?' asked Harry, who was the one most likely to succumb to such an offer.

'Ma sister, ye cooney.'

But Harry was not to be tempted. 'Nay lad, Ah said Ah'd meet oor lass oop The Rink.'

'Ad away man,' said Bob.

'Get some beer inside ye and forget the lasses, there's allus trouble whin ye ahl gan oop The Rink.'

Bob was rumoured to be suffering from heartbreak over a young woman who had jilted him for a Merchant Navy officer, but what he said was true. The arrival of a gang of unaccompanied Forge apprentices, each with a bottle of Double Maxim in his hip pocket could seriously disrupt a barn dance so that half the men found their partners taken over at the next progression. But it was mostly a good laugh just the same.

The talk went on and we got our two small tables together and by nine thirty, when there were only a few bottles left, the tide of opinion began to change, leaving Bob and Spike in a minority.

'Away man, Bob, fetch the bottles and we'l get ti t'Rink afore the doors close,' said Ginger.

The management of The Rink, a combined cinema and skating rink, put on one dance a week after scrubbing the skating floor early on Saturday evenings, and they provided a good little band but they had no bar and prohibited the import of drink by customers. The police patrolled the doors at pub closing time and they were firmly shut to those arriving after 10 p.m. We had to beat them to it, so we stowed away a bottle each, saying goodnight to Molly who had one of her fancy men with her who was leaning far over the bar towards her noted cleavage. I had two bottles for the simple reason that when I had my latest suit made the tailor kindly put in two very large hip pockets, each suited to a pint bottle. If I let my jacket swing loose I could get away with it, particularly if another apprentice stood close behind me in the queue. What my normal silhouette was like I don't know but that pair of trousers got me into many teetotal dances with the necessary smuggled alcohol; and that was one rule which clearly could not be allowed to apply to apprentice electricians. Our honour depended upon it.

On this occasion we had cut it a bit fine and we ran up the road, overtaking the police patrol about 200 yds from the entrance and just beating them to it. After paying and passing the piercing glare of the doorman, the next thing was to stow the bottles away. Walking with two bottles is awkward; trying to do the Palais Glide with them is a step towards suicide or public ignominy. The usual place to put them was immersed in the fire buckets where the level was low and the liquid so opaque that they could be sunk without trace until required. On this occasion we were baulked because the buckets had been replaced by large zinc bins and a diver would have been needed to salvage any bottle dropped in there; so I put mine on top of the lavatory cistern in one of the stalls in the gents and the others found their own suitable spots and then we went to enrich the lives of the many smart young women in the hall.

Harry hailed his sister, a most attractive girl who did not seem very pleased to see him. She was with an American sergeant and we did not particularly want any trouble with him, but she introduced us to some of her chums who also worked at the Pyrex factory and we got on with the dancing. I went out after about half an hour to get my refreshment and found the yank sergeant collapsed in the lavatory seat, rubbing his head. There was broken glass everywhere but he was not cut, just slightly stunned, and one of my bottles was missing. It was obvious what had happened but I made it up to him by offering him the first swig out of the remaining bottle. He was convinced that he had been clubbed but said, 'Thank Christ I wasn't robbed too.'

We worked out for his comfort that he had perhaps pinched somebody's girl and had been felled so that he would be out of the way. He explained that he had met her in town and taken her out to dinner that evening. We all thought he was being taken for a ride when we talked it over afterwards, and since Harry had disappeared with his sister when we came out, it was possible that Harry had come along to defend his younger sister's virginity, but even for that he would not have hit the yank, he was too kind-hearted. I went up to the outside balcony where Reggie and I finished the bottle and he then threw it over onto the railway line where it made a spectacular crash.

Another evening I picked up a girl at The Rink. I was there earlier than usual because I had been missing my usual crowd by minutes at the various pubs, yet next day they would all say, 'Ye stayed at yam all the neet then, Tom?' I had seen this girl there before, usually with a crowd of four or five people and, although we had danced, she had always gone back to her crowd. On this occasion she seemed to be alone and we were getting on well; I could dance no better than most but I was wearing light shoes and I did not tread on her feet and that was enough to shine at The Rink. I had no bottles in reserve that evening, either, so we had a few cups of tea together between dances before the kiosk closed and then there was the last waltz, always played in subdued light which created an encouraging melting feeling about the whole process. She went to get her coat and I met her in the entrance hall and we started to walk towards Grangetown.

It was always a surprise to a townie like me how far these girls expected you to walk them home at night. Three miles was nothing. I have walked for an hour and a half, and then another hour and a half back in the pitch dark before. On one occasion I suggested a taxi to hear the response, 'What, get in a cab with a lad I dinna ken? Yer cracked!' The social mores were singular. The same girl would canoodle in a pub with all the lights on, or stand on her own doorstep in the moonlight for as long as you chose to entertain her there.

On this occasion, I detected the promise of a beautiful friendship and I would have walked to Durham and back just to hold her hand; but there was a snag. Two of her usual party followed us. There had been some tiff or other, and I was just the stooge it seemed. The next thing I knew was that she screamed and I was struck in the back by what felt like a ton of coal. This was a light evening and we were walking out in the road because the pavement was obstructed by a tram queue. I fell down in the road and was jumped on for a while and I remember hearing one woman in the queue saying, 'It's arful, canna ye dee nowt, Charlie? It's a proper shyam. The poor lad!'

There were other murmurs but no one seemed to do anything. I was on my hands and knees and I remember feeling some large round horse droppings in front of my hands. I was pondering how I might perhaps spread ignominy if not pain among my attackers by throwing it at them and bringing discredit if not defeat, when I was kicked under the chin and lost all interest in any offensive. I concentrated on making myself as small as I could and rolled in amongst the tram queue. Eventually they went off and I was helped up and brushed down by the onlookers. I stopped at a public lavatory and cleaned up a bit under the tap and then went home. Nobody else was up so late at Holmlands Park and I got away with it. I saw the girl again; she was sorry about my face but not abashed at all. I was with somebody else at that time but I examined her party and could not recognise anyone. I could have arranged for a party of apprentices to do some of them over and they would have regarded it as a good evenings entertainment.

I met Reggie again, twenty years later, when he was managing the Electrical Engineering Department of the Hong Kong and Whampo Dock Company; his company were doing some repair work on a ship that I was then serving in and he invited me home for supper. His wife was that very same girl, but she did not recognise me – or did not admit to doing so, anyway – and I was not going to mention it.

Warships

Flower Class Corvette, 1941 and Castle Class Corvette, 1942

The Quair Fella transferred me to Pickersgill's to work with Stan, again at my request. I felt that I had more to offer than just lights and generators in tramp steamers and the like. I had first met Stan when he was building a Flower Class corvette a year before and for the whole of the first week I was one of thirty men there for the hauling in of the 'main run' electric cables.

These are peculiar to warships because their electrical installations are primarily for the sensors and weapons rather than just the power for various machines and devices, although that in itself is five times the quantity of that in an equivalent merchant ship hull.

We began by laying out on the jetty and measuring out about fifty different cables. Some were multicore cables with over sixty conductors inside a lead sheath and some were main power cables connecting the generators and principal power using devices to the switchboards – also lead-sheathed but single core and very much stiffer because of the large copper cores. Many of these were duplicated, one on each side of the ship. All of these cables needed to be threaded through watertight bulkheads and decks without diminishing watertightness, and that involved what was known as an admiralty pattern packing gland.

This device was a metal tube threaded at both ends and about 4 in. long. It was passed through a closely fitting hole in the bulkhead and a band of waterproofing compound spread around it, after which a washer and a nut were screwed down onto each side of the bulkhead so that the joint between the gland and the steel was watertight. Two more nuts designed to fit closely over the destined cable were then put on, one on each end of the bulkhead gland. The size of the gland was decided by the size of the cable to be passed through it, and might carry from two small cables, each about ¼ in. in diameter, up to a 2 in. diameter multicore. All of these details were shown on drawings provided to the shipbuilder by the Director General Ships Drawing Offices at Bath, Somerset.

The careful positioning and the drilling of the many holes for these glands had been arranged by Stan as soon as the bulkheads were erected and the associated perforated steel cable trays between them had been installed ready for clipping up the cables once they had been rove through the glands. All this preparatory work had been done by two apprentices and two labourers who had been with Stan since the launch three weeks before. We were the reeving gang, fleeted down by Wrightson to get the next stage completed so that the connecting-up of the many circuits could begin.

After laying out the cables, the largest one was carefully handled up from the jetty to the boiler room hatch, down the hatch and the end was then passed forward through the first bulkhead. Two or three men working on staging close up to the overhead deck in each compartment then moved it along to the next gland, supporting it all the time to prevent damage to the lead sheath as it passed slowly through the gland. This involved concerted movements by men in up to four or five compartments and was done by whistle signals given by Stan.

Once that cable had reached its furthest forward destination it was tied up to the cable tray with ropes and then the rest of that cable was rove through going aft. Eventually there was a cable running from right forward to right aft, hopefully undamaged and through all the right glands. This was then repeated for thirty or forty cables on each side of the ship, some vital cables being duplicated, one on each side, to limit action damage to the installations. A warship was expected to survive extensive damage and still to be able to fight.

The whole process took about ten days and then the work of clipping up the cables began. Brass clips shaped to a cable, or bunch of cables, were attached to the perforated steel tray by ¼ in. brass bolts and nuts, about one clip every 12 in. to 15 in. The work required two men in each compartment, usually a man and a labourer or an apprentice and a labourer. The work involved straightening and dressing the cables into an orderly bunch, sometimes twenty or more under a single clip, shaping them adequately where they entered the glands at each bulkhead. This dressing of the many cables needed to be completed throughout the length of the run before the final clipping-up could begin otherwise some cables would be stretched and some would hang in loops unless the correct lengths lay between the bulkheads. It was heavy and finicking work, and in winter involved frozen hands and some nipped fingers too. When it was done to Stan's satisfaction the 'fleeting crew' were whittled down to the number of men required to complete the installing and connecting of the cables; in this case six tradesmen and apprentices and three or four labourers. Stan asked me to stay and to take charge of the cabin lighting down aft and this I did for a week with a labourer.

This was entirely different from merchant ship work because every switch, power point and light fitting needed to be watertight and each cable had to be passed into the fitting through a watertight seal. It was again slow meticulous work, but the connecting-up was identical to merchant ships once the cable had been dressed into position, the gland made watertight and the lead sheath stripped back inside the fitting only.

After vetting my work, Stan then sent me to complete the connecting-up of the ASDIC installation cables; it was better to have one man do both ends of any cable run because then the responsibility for the finished work would be clear. Every connection would eventually be tested by a team from the Admiralty Drawing Office at Bath before the ship was accepted. After another three weeks I was sent back to Austins and re-mained with Bobby for another year.

When I rejoined Stan in 1942 I was again a part of the team hauling in cables for the first week in the new ship and then Stan sent me to work in the wireless office. Here again I was responsi-ble for the internal cabling in the office and for the various outlying parts of the ship from which the radios could be controlled such as the cypher office, the bridge and the emer-gency conning position aft.

I had another apprentice, junior to me, who worked under my direction and we got along well enough as he was keen to learn. I often got talking to the standby naval people who joined the ship as work progressed; there were engine room artificers and an engineer officer, some seamen petty officers and torpedomen who looked after the electrical equipment at that time. Mostly I spoke with the petty officer telegraphist (PO Tel) whose gear I was working on in the wireless office. This was a large compartment in the middle of the superstructure and directly below the mast where the aerials were all mounted; it contained eight or nine transmitters and many receivers. All of these worked on 230 v AC and required a special motor alternator for their operation because the main electrical power was 220 v DC. The motor alternator, one of two available, was sited low down in the ship in a space called the low power room where there were many different motor alternators serving the many special systems installed. As each area of the office was finished the PO Tel switched on and tested out his units.

Towards the end the completed gear included a TBS, which was a short-range medium frequency radio telephone with which he used to call up weather forecasts and chat with the other operators. There was no security hazard here; the frequencies were for port use only and by choice of words would yield no direct information to a listener, and its range was limited to a few miles anyway. Any data of significance was not sent by voice but by encrypted Morse code, a special typewriter called a Typex, similar to the German Enigma, being used to encode the signal before transmission. The Typex produced a perforated paper tape which was then fed to an automatic transmitter and the message was sent out at very high speed, far faster than any telegraphist could handle his Morse key.

One day he called up the weather station and a woman's voice replied crisply, 'Newcastle HQ.'

'Party Sparkers,' he said to me later. 'It's nice to hear their little voices when you are out on the hogwash.'

'Who are they, PO?' I asked.

'Wrens,' he said. 'Very select, they are, you know; not just anyone gets into the Wrens. Cream of society, they are. No dumb blondes either – they are crackers when the heat is on. Gives you real confidence to hear them all calm and speaking clear and slow.'

Huff Duff

The Castle Class corvette from Pickersgill's yard sailed in November 1942 and, I believe, survived the war to be put into reserve in 1946. My final job in her was the 'huff duff' or high frequency direction-finding (HF/DF) set called the FH4. This was the equipment which could pick up a submarine transmission instantly; if two ships caught it they could plot its position by cross bearings and begin to 'home in' the other escorts onto it within minutes. It had a range of about 30 miles when working well and a group of escorts could span a large area of ocean around the convoy. This long range and its sensitivity depended upon a large, specialised two-channel, five-stage receiver in the main office and, from this, four large, very low impedance cables covered with a copper wire braid and a tarred jute serving were led straight up the mast and then to a special 10 ft topmast, on which rested a fantastic birdcage aerial. This was a very recognisable feature of all these latest corvettes and frigates; it was about 6 ft high and 3 ft square in plan, made up of pieces of varnished wood and cast aluminium corner joints.

This frame carried two loop wire aerials at right angles plus a short spike on the top called a 'sense aerial'. These actual aerial wires were buried within the cage structure but their connections came down to two large junction boxes on the metal base of the aerial and right at the top of the 4 in. diameter steel tube topmast. The four cables were required to be exactly the same 'electrical length' to within a few units of impedance and therefore initially of identical physical lengths to a millimetre.

All this was explained to me by a lieutenant from the Royal Navy Volunteer Reserve (RNVR) who came down to bring the secret documents associated with the set. I was not allowed to see these documents. They went to the confidential book safe where the PO Tel could consult them if I asked him for any data, but the officer gave me the essential installation details to write in my notebook. I had assistance from another apprentice and a labourer to measure and clip up these vital cables and the naval officer advised me to cut off some 10 in. lengths and to practise several times the method of connection before starting on the real ones; I soon found out why. Inside the jute wrap and outside the copper braided sheath was a wax-impregnated cotton layer. Following his drawing, I cut back the jute, cut back the cotton, both for 4 in. plus 50 mm and left all their ends smooth and tidy. This revealed the braided copper sheath. I measured back 4 in. plus 30 mm of braided sheath and cut it carefully with snips, strand by strand removing the unwanted part; this left a piece about 4 in. long exposed. This 4 in. of the active part of the special cable was the part which emerged into the connection box both at the receiver in the office and up on the topmast. It was about as thick as your middle finger and looked like candle wax, it melted like it too which he had warned me about. Despite this, 1 in. of it had to be removed to expose a large copper conductor about 4 mm thick. This needed to be soldered into a brass connector which was then bolted onto the connection block inside the special junction boxes.

The process of melting the solder and tinning the copper without also melting the candle wax insulation required some trial and error with my blowlamp. I eventually got the hang of it and the most important thing was not to move either the copper or the wax during the heating process. Some cooling materials could also be wrapped round the wax; nothing wet was allowed but metal foil and a rubber bag containing ice cubes from the galley helped.

Thanks to the initial practice on scrap bits I managed to connect the four cables in the office without destroying them and then I had my real test – 60 ft up in the air, standing on two narrow steel steps with a safety belt holding me from falling while I used two hands on each of the cables up there. It took me two hours to do the first one and I came down with chattering teeth because the December wind was icy. It helped to keep the wax cool but did not improve my dexterity with pliers, hacksaw, blowlamp and solder!

After warming myself I went back up and did another one

before dinner. Then it came on to snow and I decided that wet was not good for junction boxes and closed the lot up for the night and wrapped the two remaining cable ends in rubber tape.

The next day I managed two more and came down feeling highly satisfied with my week's work, especially when the overall test with a meter showed that the essential limiting values of impedance had been preserved for all four cables.

That afternoon the ship was required to be towed down to the South Dock for the 4 in. gun to be lifted onto the forecastle deck, and the pilot was anxious to get her down there before dark and perhaps he hurried things along before the tide was exactly right or perhaps no one had told him about the extra 15 ft on top of the mast. Whatever it was, blast his eyes, he got it wrong, and as the ship went under Monkwearmouth Bridge the aerial struck the bridge and collapsed into a heap of broken wood.

After we arrived in the South Docks and secured below the large crane, a new aerial was found. I stripped away the old one and the next day the new one was lifted up by crane and secured by the shipwright. It took me three days to connect it this time because the berth was so exposed that I could work for only an hour at a time before freezing solid in the icy wind; however I did not need to resolder anything as the lugs with the cables were exactly right for the new aerial – as everyone but me had confidently assumed.

The tests were once again satisfactory and the PO Tel seemed content and was waiting his opportunity during sea trials to get the whole set calibrated and 'swung'. Like any electronic device the bearing recorded by the device was in error for all relative bearings because of the reflections peculiar to each ship installation. The reflections could come from neighbouring steel structures, from the funnel and funnel stay wires, from any other aerials and so on. This requires the ship to be held at anchor at a special berth, from which a standard signal can be heard from a transmitter on shore on a known compass bearing from the berth. Then, while the stern is towed round in a circle, the bearing recorded by the FH4 display was plotted against the actual bearing of the transmitter and a deviation chart produced. Then, when a U-boat was heard on some bearing registered by the FH4, the true relative bearing from the ship could be plotted from the deviation chart. Strictly, a deviation for every degree was needed but when it became obvious that for certain sectors, mainly abeam, the error was very small, the PO would skip a few to get the job done as it was done afresh for each frequency band, perhaps ten bands in all. But I was not there to see it.

Getting Away

In the spring of 1943 I sat for my Higher National Certificate exam; I would not know until September whether or not I had passed but I felt confident. From 8 February 1942 I had been on a man's rate of pay. I had been interviewed by Mr Gurney, the manager, on coming out of my time and he completed my indenture as he had promised.

I told him of my confidence in the exam result and he said, 'We canna pay ye moor fer ye certificate but we can make sure ye get the jobs which carry extra allowances. When ye get yer certificate I will send ye ower to Thompson's Yard as a marker-off and that pays four pence an hour extra.'

I went on with my work at Pickersgill's yard with Stan for the next five months, working on two more warships which completed the run of corvettes of the Castle Class. I worked on all systems, the Squid mortar, the ASDIC and several more wireless offices with their FH4 installations with which I was now considered to be the expert. The next jobs would be Bird Class sloops and I looked forward to this change of style because they would be primarily anti-aircraft ships with a powerful gun armament.

But before they began I was sent down to Thompson's as Wrightson had predicted. There I joined a team building a long programme of the standardised ships of 9000 tonnes as designed by Kaiser for mass production in the USA. We all agreed that Thompson's had provided the original design of the Liberty Ship which Kaiser had then re-engineered to suit his brief for mass production using prefabrication processes. We were now in turn adopting these so far as practicable in our crowded riverside yards, supported by green field prefabrication sites up to ten miles away from the river.

At Thompson's I found a tough old man of sixty called Jim Frame who was the ship chargeman. He had two labourers and now had me as his marker-off. Between us we had to lay out the ship installation working from the available drawings and see to it that all necessary welding, drilling, cooperation with other departments on layout, batches of work and appropriate supplies were available or ordered to match the increasing numbers of men who would be fleeted down from other yards as the work progressed. I was the chargeman's doggy in other words; he did the difficult bits and I did the simple, boring bits. In a small ship the chargeman does it all as Bobby Potts did in Austins, but as this much larger and more complex ship progressed there would eventually be four marker-offs, each with a specific area of responsibility.

The Chinese Prince

The particular ship being fitted out when I arrived was the *Chinese Prince*: not a standard cargo ship of 9000 tonnes such as they usually built but a fast cargo and passenger ship of 11,000 tonnes intended to run the Atlantic without a convoy. She was therefore rather special. In addition to helping Jim with the general layout of the cabling through the ship I was to start with responsibility for the upper deck cabins, then the bridge superstructure as it was erected and finally the equipment mounted there such as ASDIC, RDF and radio. A nice package of work, I thought. The two labourers were making sample steel cable clips for the heaviest cables under Jim's direction and sending them up to the Forge to be made in tens or hundreds, depending upon the cable runs involved. Jim was driving them along and he drove me too.

'This is a special ship and yer job has to be done right. The distribution system in the superstructure is unique and involves a 220 v DC ring main system round all the cabins; de ye understand that?'

I assured him that I did; it had been one of the methods used at Pinewood Film Studios in 1939, only on that occasion it was 230 v AC. There were no differences technically.

'The advantage for ye is that each cabin has a fuse outside in the passage and so it can be wired up as a separate unit. Because of that I will use yer cabin accommodation as a float job and any man with an hour to spare will be sent to ye to do a little bit. Can ye manage that?'

I said that I could, although I could foresee some struggles arising from time to time. However, I was paid four pence an hour for such trouble and on a hundred hours each week that was a consideration. I would be able to work out some recognisable system for controlling this technically minor part of my work.

'Because of this ring main ye needna' wayt for the cabins to be built, ye can run yer ring main aroond now in the passage behind the false ceiling and leave a loop down at each cabin door position for clipping up later; very easy that will be and each cabin can be tested before ye connect it to the ring to bowl out the bad work.'

I knew what he meant; I would get the least useful people and would need to check everything that they did.

'By the way, ye'll have two women dilutee electricians as yer permanent staff from tomorrow. One can run a storeroom for yer minor gear and the other can keep the job rolling along under your eye, clear up loose ends and so on. Will that suit ye?'

He had a glint in his eye as he said this and I had some entrancing visions myself – but I had not then met Bella. Bella came first and she was a tall blonde wearing a leopard skin coat; she was single, as hard as nails and she stank. Looking back, I suppose that I should have hit her hard between the eyes on that first meeting and avoided trouble thereafter but I was green then and hitting women was not accepted in my world. As it was she walked round the cabin deck with me, listened to my instructions and then disappeared. I did not go round again for two days and when I did I found nothing had been done and tackled her about it. She was sitting chatting to a plumber and smoking his cigarettes in a languid manner.

'Ah'll dee yerr work when ye ask me nicely. Kiss my ass for a starter.'

I was clearly out of my depth here, I temporised.

'You can do the work or not as you wish but your pay is docked if it's not done by the end of the week.'

I told Jim what had occurred and he said give her the week. She did no work, got no pay from us and left the ship; I never saw her again but I heard the odd gossip about the 'piece with the leopard skin coat' who was still apparently employed by somebody at the Forge.

Doreen arrived next. She was fortyish, married (her husband was a sergeant in North Africa) and she was willing to do any job that she was given; willing, but not very able. She could make a tangle out of any two wires in a compartment; she could cut them off short when I had left them long; she could even wire up the wrong cabin where some of the wooden bulkheads were missing and where no electrical work should have been started. She was very efficient as my storekeeper, tea-maker and holder of my chalk line; she was totally loyal and kept good track of the paperwork for ordering stores and recording who had used them when the busy times came. She should have been employed as a labourer not a dilutee electrician, but who cared? We worked it out well between us and we got along fine.

When the next woman arrived to take Bella's place she was also in her forties and married with a soldier husband but very competent at her electrician's work. Doreen kept her fully employed and I had little contact with her; perhaps Doreen should have been the marker-off, not me?

As Jim had said, there were ten men working for me one day and two or none the next. Halfway through the job the yard was bombed; one bomb fell in the river close to the ship and all the wooden cabin bulkheads fell down carrying my wiring with them. That meant a whole month's work to do again and Doreen arranged for most of it. I was by then engrossed in my bridge equipment, wireless, ASDIC and RDF which were in the steel structure and not affected by the blast. Then, in September, I received my exam result; I had passed well in all subjects.

I was less concerned that I had justified Gurney's selection of me as a marker-off (although the certificate now justified the extra pay), than with the fact that I had now fully discharged my undertaking to my father. I was a qualified electrical engineer, a student member of the Institution of Electrical Engineers and, following suitable experience, eligible to be an associate member of this most prestigious technical body. Now I wanted to get away from shipbuilding which, productive and important as it was to the war effort, was not my idea of a lifetime career. I had written to the Joint Recruiting Board in Newcastle in May and was then told to write again when I had my exam result. I now sent off a card to the Joint Recruiting Board and a week later I received a letter to go to Newcastle for an interview and I went to ask Jim for time off.

'I knew all ye cockneys were bluidy mad, ye moos be raevin to volunteer for that lot. What's wrang wi this job? Divn't we please ye here?'

There was no logical answer to that so I just said something about being young and fit and leaving quiet numbers like Thompson's to old bastards like him which he took in good part.

The Joint Recruiting Board interview was short and concerned only my qualifications. I had taken along my National and Higher National Certificates as asked, and my indenture endorsed by Gurney in September 1942, plus my identity card to ensure that they were talking to the right bloke. I was quizzed about the work that I had been doing and was told that there were vacancies in the REME, the RAF Technical Branch or in the Naval Electrical Branch, any of which would suit my technical ability and experience.

Which did I prefer? Once again I should have anticipated the question, but had given it little thought. Without a moment's hesitation and again relying upon intuition I said, 'The Navy.'

I thought during the rest of that day of the little that I knew of the Navy. What did they do with their electricians? Would I be doing the same work as now for a fraction of the pay and being bawled at by petty officers? Would I go to sea in some unimagined capacity with a blown-up lifebelt and looking grim over cocoa in the middle watch? I did not find out for certain for months. My mother's reaction I do not now remember; my mates said little but clearly thought that I had a screw loose. They failed to see that I was as much 'away from home' in Sunderland as I could ever be in the forces. True, I slept in a house and had a mother and brother living in the same house, but otherwise there was nothing but my never-ending work and my boozing mates on a Saturday night. I felt that I could be happy anywhere that was warm in winter.

The SS *Chinese Prince* progressed and became more like a ship, with very good lines and good quality work throughout. The RDF hut (later to be called radar) was lifted on to the top of the bridge structure and I began to wire it into the ship. It was a pre-fabricated set called a 271MX and it was a merchant ship adaptation of a new type of 10 cm set usable for warning against either ships or aircraft out to about 25 miles in ideal conditions. The average detection range was 15 miles I was told by a young lieutenant in the RNVR who came to inspect. I had made one or two guesses about various parts of the equipment and he confirmed these and gossiped generally about RDF.

I told him that I had volunteered for the Navy and he congratulated me and told me that he was a Faraday House Apprentice and had entered the RNVR directly as an officer about a year before. He assured me that with my qualifications I too would be entered directly as an RNVR officer if I was medically fit and that after that I could be sent anywhere. This was an entirely new dimension to my future and I pondered for a long time; surely a naval officer would have been able to deal with Bella? What did I know which would compare with the breadth of experience of that PO Tel in the Castle Class corvette at Pickersgill's? I both liked and distrusted the idea, but I told no one. For me, the prospect foretold yet another complete break with everything that I knew and was familiar with; for the third time in my short life I was accepting a step into a strange world with a new language and different values. It had always been a lonely business and now I had to foresee it again, but I never had any doubt that I would take the chance now that it had come.

My speculation was interrupted by another air raid. When I arrived one October morning the big travelling crane with rails on the quay was lying across the bridge structure and my radar hut was squashed flat. The ship's hull was full of holes and she lay on the bottom with a pronounced list to starboard, leaning away from the quay and sustained only by ropes. The shipwrights said she would have sunk if she had not sat on the muddy bottom. So we began again and by mid-November she was again afloat, her bottom and sides repaired by divers, her cables replaced or jointed. These apparently special attacks on her encouraged us to get her done and off to sea, as Hitler clearly feared her potential.

In early December I was called to London for an interview and went to Number 36 Whitehall, which was soon to become familiar. I was ushered into a waiting room with a lot of serious young men. We were counted by a civilian and named against his list, then put into a bus and taken to Queen Anne's Mansions where a series of medical and other tests were applied to us.

'Pee in that bottle, blow into that pipe, take your shirt off and breathe deeply, stand on one leg… Hop, keep hopping, higher… Can you see any pattern in this blob of ink? In this group of dots?'

Then back to 36 Whitehall by bus and more waiting. Finally, the call came. 'Mr Gilbert, please.'

I walked into a room which looked as large as a barn but whose details did not register otherwise. There was a green baize-covered table in front of me with four men sitting at it in dark blue uniforms with gold braid on their sleeves.

'Sit down there, please, Mr Gilbert.'

I walked across to the chair with what aplomb I could muster.

'Like walking out to bat. Eh?'

He meant well, but I didn't dare say that I hadn't played cricket for ten years and even then the games did not last long enough to let me into the batting order. So I just mumbled agreement. They asked me very simple questions on electrical matters, mostly about car electrics; nothing about ships, nothing about real electrical engineering as I understood it, just magnetos and batteries – things I had played with as a schoolboy. Then it was over and I went out, confirming my address with the civilian who was holding the list. I walked to Charing Cross Station for my bag, took the underground to King's Cross and the train back to Sunderland.

I was now very much aware that I wanted to leave Sunderland. I had worked flat out from the day that I had arrived in September 1940, like everybody else there, and it was now over three years later. Every weekday of that period I had either worked overtime to 9 p.m. or been at college to 9.30 p.m. and on Sundays I had homework which lasted until as late as 10 or 11 p.m. I knew that I had thereby struggled several important rungs up the technical ladder and that my experience of electrical installation work was extensive, probably uniquely so, and that I was good at it, much better than most without being too cocky. I felt that my contribution to 'the war effort' was by no means negligible and that by volunteering for the Navy I was likely to go further to promote it. I knew that I was nowhere near extended either by my technical or practical work and that I had untried reserves of learning ability available and a sound technical base for further study should it be offered to me. The best that could happen to me in Sunderland was that I could become a chargeman like Stan and go on with much the same sort of work until I retired or was fired.

It was time to go, despite my many friendships and the many sterling men I had got to know in that fearfully cold place called Wearside.

Printed in the United States
205586BV00001B/112/A